Engage   Explain   Encourage

Achieve effective exposure control

Improving Efficiency and Effectiveness of

COSHH-Risk Management

A practical companion for occupational safety and health practitioners

Making it Easy for You

Making it Easy for Your Colleagues

Dr Bob Rajan – Rajadurai Sithamparanadarajah OBE JP

Disclaimer

The information contained within this publication was obtained from reliable sources and/or drawn from the experiences of the author. However, whilst every effort has been made to ensure its accuracy, no responsibility for loss, damage, or injury occasioned to any person acting or refraining from action as a result of information contained herein cannot be accepted by the author. Any opinions, views, recommendations and/or conclusions expressed are those of the author alone and do not necessarily reflect the policies of any organisation referenced or mentioned in this book.

This book contains public sector information licensed under the Open Government Licence v3.0. Several visual aids (with source references, where applicable) are used in this book to aid improved communication, many of these carry Crown Copyright.

Contents

Dedication i

Acknowledgements ii

About the Author iii

About the book iv

Abbreviations vii

Foreword ix

Messages Of Support And Good Wishes xi

Chapter 1: Controlling Exposure to Hazardous Substances at Work 1

1.1 Thoughts and work of Hippocrates and Ramazzini 1

1.2 Developments in Great Britain (GB) 1

1.3 The Control of Substances Hazardous to Health (COSHH) Regulations 3

1.4 What is a substance hazardous to health (SHH)? 3

1.5 Prevention, substitution and adequate control 8

1.6 Measures to be taken for achieving adequate control of exposure 9

1.7 The test for adequate control of exposure 12

1.8 The "principles of good practice." 12

1.9 Undertaking work involving SHH 14

1.10 Controlling exposure to SHH so far, a brief summary 15

1.11 Proportionate work remains to further reduce the extent of exposure 18

1.12 Summary 21

Chapter 2: Contexts for Helping to Deliver Good Control Practice 22

2.1 Introduction 22

2.2 Exploring proportionate risk management 22

2.3. Examples of proportionality-related issues 24

2.4 Occupational health statistics 29

2.5 HSE and HM Courts activities 30

2.6 Work-related lung diseases, HSE's priorities 33

2.7 Needs of SMEs and the frontline 33

2.8 Summary 35

Chapter 3: Challenges and Failures 36

3.1 Introduction 36

3.2 Long latency and work-related ill health 36

3.3 Risk sharing and transfer 39

3.4 Self-employed and COSHH 41

3.5 Extent of COSHH awareness 41

3.6 Potential scarcity of competent designers 42

3.7 OSH Admin failures 42

3.8 Designing exposure controls and consultation with operatives 43

3.9 'Unworried'/unaware workers 43

3.10 Blaming employees for control failures 45

3.11 OSH consultants' points of view 47

3.12 Consultants and suppliers and their advice 48

3.13 Educate and empower the next generation of workers and managers 48

3.14 Management hesitancy 48

3.15 Trainers and trainees' preferences 49

3.16 Inadequate exposure control designs 49

3.17 PPE as the first line of exposure control 50

3.18 Summary 50

Chapter 4: An Introduction to Training on Risk Awareness and Undertaking Risk Assessments 51

4.1 Introduction 51

4.2 Essential steps for safe working with substances hazardous to health 52

4.3 A simple dashboard introducing OSH-RM concepts 54

4.4 Health Risks at Work. Do you know yours? 55

4.5 Learning Occupational Health by Experiencing Risks (LOcHER) 55

4.6 An introduction to understanding risk 56

4.7 An introduction to risk ranking 61

4.8 A case study introduction to risk assessment 63

4.9 Other risk assessment tools 65

4.10 COSHH Essentials direct advice sheets 65

4.11 When using COSHH Essentials direct advice sheets 67

4.12 Examples of potential consequences of incorrect decisions made when designing, installing and using control measures 70

4.13 A description of the principles underpinning the COSHH Control Banding approach for inhalation exposure control 77

4.14 A worked example using the paper-based CB 84

4.15 COSHH control banding e-tool 87

4.16 HSE's RA template 88

4.17 Summary 89

Chapter 5 Local Exhaust Ventilation in COSHH Risk Management 90

5.1 Introduction 90

5.2 Understanding sucking and blowing in ventilation systems 91

5.3 Contaminant capture zone 91

5.4 A poor understanding of capture zone 94

5.5 Fast moving contaminant clouds and inefficient control 95

5.6 Vapour is heavier than air, misconception 96

5.7 Missing importance sources of exposure 97

5.8 Operator standing in the wrong place 99

5.9 Head in contaminated air 100

5.10 One size hood fit for all 101

5.11 Substance is not classified as hazardous by the GHS system, no need for LEV 103

5.12 Barbecue smoke effect 104

5.13 Working in the open air, no need for LEV 106

5.14 General ventilation 107

5.15 A list of examples of problems associated with incorrect LEV operation 108

5.16 Summary 109

Chapter 6 Respiratory Protective Equipment (RPE) and COSHH Risk Management 111

6.1 Introduction 111

6.2 RPE selection 112

6.3 Incorrect selection of RPE 115

6.4 Examples of other issues with RPE use 117

6.5 Summary 120

Chapter 7: Skin Exposure to Substances Hazardous to Health and Its Control 123

7.1 Skin Exposure at work 123

7.2 Dynamics of skin exposure 123

7.3 Skin exposure pathways 126

7.4 Applying safe working distance (SWD) for avoiding skin exposure.............................129

7.5 Technology and skin exposure control...130

7.6 Summary 133

Chapter 8: Leading Indicators for Determining Exposure Control Effectiveness.....................134

8.1 Introduction 134

8.2 A headline introduction to leading indicators 135

8.3 Developing and using leading Exposure Control Indicators (ECIs) in COSHH-RM.......135

8.4 About ECIs..136

8.5 A summary of desirable usability characteristics of codified ECIs with BMs 137

8.6 A list of COSHH-ECIs..138

8.7 Summary 138

Appendix 8.1 139

Appendix 8.2 142

Chapter 9: Efficient and Effective Decision Making..147

9.1 Introduction 147

9.2 Efficiency and effectiveness..147

9.3 At the "coalface" 148

9.4 Competence and prudence 149

9.5 A suggestion for assessing the effectiveness of OSH delivery 150

9.6 Anticipating inspectors' expectations 152

9.7 Summary 153

Chapter 10: Inspiring OSH Buy-In By Operational Management..155

10.1 Introduction 155

10.2 Becoming an OSH salesperson 156

10.3 What does it entail?..156

10.4 Building finance into OSH 157

10.5 Examples of financial terms..159

10.6 A hypothetical example on OSH perspective and OSH buy-in 161

10.7 Summary 164

Chapter 11: Make It Happen..165

11.1 Introduction 165

11.2 Basics of communication, Cs in communication and anchoring 166

11.3 Communication and OSH goals...166

11. 4 Risk Communication.. 167

11.5 OSH-RM communication purposes 168

11.6 Key elements involved in effective RM communication............................ 168

11.7 Putting into practice – an example risk communication 170

11.8 Nudging for influencing better behaviours 172

11.9 Summary 178

Concluding remarks... 179

References.. 180

Index 198

Dedication

This book is dedicated to my beloved brother, late Babu and my greatly valued colleague and friend, late Carolyn Creed.

Babu, you had been a delight, and your smile made our hearts bloom. When I see a bird chirping in my garden, I will think of your funny words! You will always live in our thoughts.

Carolyn joined RoSPA in 2016 from a background in public relations and community engagement. She used these strengths to both maintain and evolve relationships between SGUK and other RoSPA networks, supporting SGUK trustees, and the groups network. Her ability to put people at ease, in addition to being open and collaborative, added great value to the work of SGUK. The network continues to benefit from her work, a golden thread during her time with SGUK.

Acknowledgements

Alone I can achieve a little; together, we can achieve so much more.

With thanks to my fellow professionals - my teachers, OSH practitioners, researchers, scientists, strategists, policy makers, inspectors - and friends.

When I thought of writing this book, Karen McDonnell of RoSPA regularly nudged me to persevere. I am delighted that the book has taken the shape to be a companion for OSH practitioners.

I am most grateful to John Cherrie and Diane Llewellyn for their carefully calibrated comments and suggestions on the drafts of this book, which were invaluable in developing this companion. My sincere thanks to Robert Atkinson, Mike Calcutt, John McAlinden, Mary and John Navaratanam, Michael Sherer, and Mahathevan Sriharan for their suggestions and comments.

Without a doubt, this book is immensely enriched by John Cherrie's Foreword and the messages of support and good wishes from Dee Arp, Kevin Bampton, Louise Hosking, Chris Keen, Alan Murray, Duncan Smith, Norman Stevenson and Errol Taylor. Thank you all.

I am glad that the book has passed with colours, the 'readers-test' undertaken by Robert Atkinson, Andy Cathro, John Cairns, Dave Foy, Gregor McGhee, Joanne Shepherd and John Thompson.

The efforts of many have been converted into an attractive publication to read and use with the careful and dedicated support of my colleagues Cheryl Ann, Michelle Mulheron, and Ruth Rivers at Amazon Publishing Pros.

This book would not have been completed without the support of my dear wife, Sumi and our children, Jonathan and Michelle, for which I am delightfully happy.

In summary, I am grateful to every one of you who contributed in your own ways to make this book a real companion for OSH practitioners.

Finally, I want to thank my readers, the most precious, for making use of this book to support proportionate, nonbureaucratic, effective and efficient COSHH-RM, and for winning the hearts and minds of employers and those potentially at risk of exposure to substances hazardous to health.

About the Author

Bob Rajan-Rajadurai Sithamparanadarajah OBE JP

Bob is a strategist, and a policy developer recently retired from the UK HSE. Bob was Awarded OBE by Her late Majesty The Queen for his services to the Department of Works and Pensions. He and his innovative strategic approaches won many awards and accolades, including the BOHS-Peter Isaac Award, the BSIF-Outstanding Contribution Award and the RoSPA-Distinguished Service Award. He contributed to the development of the British chemical exposure control regulations and authored or contributed to many publications produced by HSE and a small number of international standards. He published over thirty peer-reviewed papers in international journals, many of which are strategic in nature. Bob also edited and authored numerous articles for professional and technical magazines and had authored or contributed to professional books. He was a visiting lecturer at universities and an external examiner for PhD submissions and examinations conducted by professional bodies. He is currently Vice Chair of SGUK and a Past President of the Royal Chartered BOHS. Bob is a keen supporter of charitable activities.

About the book

As an occupational safety and health (OSH) practitioner, you will find this downloadable practical electronic book (paperback available) **a beneficial companion in your Control of Substances Hazardous to Health (COSHH) risk management (RM) activities,** including occupational safety and health knowledge exploration (OSHKE). It is written to support your own efforts in planning (**Plan**), implementing (**Do**), and monitoring (**Check**) exposure control measures, as well as reviewing and rectifying any shortfalls (**Act**). You are encouraged to use this book in conjunction with Health and Safety Executive (HSE) publications relevant to your work activities and to suit the operational environment.

Furthermore, this book should help when you are working and interacting with people who have different outlooks on OSH-RM, and you are aspiring to maximise your professional efforts as a:

-   **Change agent** for improving exposure controls measures;
-   **Implementer**, initiator and/or innovator of suitable and adequate exposure control approaches;
-   Measured **Risk taker** for getting the right things done;
-   **Catalyst** for positive change;
-   Proactive **Unifying force** on OSH matters; and
-   **Success maker** overall.

(Spot the built-in acronym in the list of bulleted words? Does it have any resemblance to the work you do?)

Those preparing for OSH qualifications and academic/OSH training institutions will find this book a handy resource.

I have translated my "beneficial companion" mission into two primary aims for this book:

- **Helping to make your job easy, and**

- **Helping you to: engage, explain, encourage and positively nudge colleagues to improve exposure control decision making;** support good industrial relations and return on investment (RoI).

It would mean effective and efficient OSH practitioners will always have in mind curiosity, proportionality, prudence, productivity, good practice, effective risk communication, nudging and selling OSH to operations. Therefore, your goals and aspirations for promoting and supporting effective OSH-RM is likely to rely heavily on:

- Progressive development and the availability of a mixture of sound academic knowledge, practical technical solutions, good practice guides, and standards,
- The application of sound knowledge, skills, training, experience and positive attitudes, including the use of appropriate techniques, tools and good quality persuasive communication, and
- The operational environments of organisations.

To help make your job easy and for helping you to engage, explain and encourage colleagues, I have condensed the knowledge of:

- The collaborative and progressive thinking of many hundreds of colleagues and organisations across different fields of expertise, and
- The 'coalface' experiences of occupational hygienists and other OSH practitioners.

This condensed knowledgebase is delivered, as much as possible, through situations-based:

- Practical examples;
- Discussions on strengths and weaknesses associated with selected COSHH-RM efforts;
- Suggestions for improving COSHH-RM;
- Visual approaches for explaining RM issues;
- Case studies for explaining RM issues;
- Learning occupational health by experiencing risks (LOcHER) demonstrations;

- Exercises to check your understanding and views of selected issues.

They are presented whenever a pertinent COSHH-RM issue is raised anywhere in the book and are constructed using the FABRIC principle set out below.

- **Focussed** on what is necessary rather than what is possible;
- **Appropriate** for work-related health risks reduction;
- **Balanced** to the needs of the practitioners and people who are exposed to SHH;
- **Realistic** enough to stand the test of time;
- **Implementable** within the intended work environment;
- **Cost effective** to implement, monitor, review and act.

(These guiding principles were synthesised based on the information in "Choosing the Right FABRIC – a framework for performance information" published by the British National Audit Office.)

The total package is delivered through OSH practitioner centred eleven Chapters, using over 100 visuals, sixty-nine Figures, twenty Tables, several LOcHER style practical demonstrations and over fifty OSHKE challenges.

Finally, two things. First, as GB is getting ready to celebrate fifty years of the world leading 'Health and Safety at Work Act', this book contributes to that celebration. Second, this book was born, like many of my strategic initiatives, from my childhood aspirations based on late President John F Kennedy's quote – "Ask not what your country can do for you; ask what you can do for your country".

Abbreviations

μm	micrometre
ACoP	Approved Code of Practice
AIDA	Awareness, Interest, Desire, Action
APF	Assigned Protection Factor
BA	Breathing apparatus
BOHS	British Occupational Hygiene Society
BSIF	British Safety Industry Federation
BZ	Breathing zone
CA	Control approaches
CB	Control banding
CE	COSHH-Essentials
COSHH	Control of Substances Hazardous to Health Regulations
CP	Competent person
CPD	Continuous professional development
CS	Confined space
DEEE	Diesel engine exhaust emissions
DIY	Do-It-Yourself
ECI	Exposure control indicator
GB	Great Britain (England, Scotland, Wales)
GHS	Globally Harmonised Scheme
HHG	Health Hazard Group
HSE	Health and Safety Executive
HSWA	Health and Safety at Work Act
IN	Improvement Notice
IOM	Institute of Occupational Medicine
IOSH	Institute of Occupational Safety and Health
ISO	International Standards Organisation
LEV	Local exhaust ventilation
LOcHER	Learning Occupational Health by Experiencing Risks
NDM	Nuisance dust mask
NEBOSH	National Examination Board in Occupational Safety and Health
OM	Operational management
OSH	Occupational safety and health
OSHCR	Occupational Safety and Health Consultants Register
OSHKE	Occupational safety and health knowledge exploration
PN	Prohibition Notice
PPE	Personal protective equipment
ppm	Parts per million
RA	Risk assessment
RIDDOR	Reporting of Injuries, Diseases & Dangerous Occurrences Regulations
RM	Risk management
RoI	Return on investment

RoSPA	The Royal Society for the Prevention of Accidents
RPE	Respiratory protective equipment
SGUK	Safety Groups UK
SHH	Substances hazardous to health
SME	Small and medium sized enterprise
SWD	Safe working distance
SWL	Safe working load
TExT	Thorough Examination and Testing of LEV
TWA	Time weighted average
UK	United Kingdom
WEL	Workplace exposure limits

Foreword

The COSHH Regulations came into force 1st of October 1989. When they were first introduced, they provided a new approach to managing the health risks from the use of substances hazardous to health at work. Employers were given the responsibility of assessing the risks for their situations and, if necessary, choosing the most appropriate strategy to eliminate or adequately control these risks. In retrospect, it is perhaps unsurprising that at this point, the quality and quantity of specific guidance on how to comply was limited. Employers did their best, but many struggled; some focused on the hazard of the chemicals and did not properly think about the way they were used, and others implemented what they thought were the necessary control measures but without any evidence of whether they were sufficient. As time has passed, we have acquired a much better understanding of how to implement the Regulations. The Health and Safety Executive has produced an enormous amount of specific guidance on the Regulations and developed strategies and tools that make it clear to employers what needs to be done. One of the key people at HSE who championed this guidance was Dr Bob Rajan.

I have known Bob for more than thirty years. I worked as a teacher and research human exposure scientist, in universities and at the Institute of Occupational Medicine in Edinburgh. Bob and I didn't work directly together, but we have been colleagues and friends through the British Occupational Hygiene Society (BOHS), meeting regularly at conferences and other events. My main connection with him has been through our common interest in protecting workers from skin exposure to chemicals. Bob led the HSEs response to occupational hygiene aspects of dermal exposure, bringing forward several innovative ideas and engaging ways to communicate the message about how best to manage these risks. We collaborated on campaigns run by Safety Groups UK, of which Bob is a Vice Chair. Bob has also been heavily involved in the LOcHER project – Learning Occupational Health through Experiencing Risks, which is designed to help vocational students/apprentices protect their future health and safety in college and on entering the world of work. Bob is an enthusiastic communicator who is constantly seeking out ways to get the message across to those who need to hear it. He read and commented on the textbook I wrote – Monitoring for Health Hazards at Work, and I have reciprocated by reading this book and giving my advice, for what it's worth, to him.

For me, this book reflects on Bob's approach to occupational health and hygiene – it truly is a practical companion for you to help achieve effective risk management within the COSHH Regulations. It is written in a conversational style with helpful additional information added to the text in breakout boxes. The material is written around the wealth of guidance material that is now available through the HSEs website, much of which Bob had a hand in writing. As might be expected, there are chapters in the book that discuss risk assessment and control of exposures using local exhaust ventilation and personal protective equipment. However, Bob has also tried to provide a perspective on how best to engage with managers in getting COSHH done – so there are chapters on 'Efficient and effective decision making' and 'Inspiring OSH buy-in by operational management.' Unsurprisingly, given Bob's interest in controlling dermal exposure, there is a complete chapter devoted to 'Skin exposure to substances hazardous to health and its control.'

I heartily recommend this book. It should provide, as the author intended, a way to make it easy for you to implement effective COSHH management systems and easy for your colleagues to understand what you are seeking to achieve.

John Cherrie

Emeritus Professor of Human Health, Heriot Watt University

and

Retired Research Director at the Institute of Occupational Medicine (IOM)

Messages Of Support And Good Wishes

From the President, British Occupational Hygiene Society (BOHS)

I've known Bob for over a quarter of a century now and have had the privilege to work alongside him many times. His 'thinking outside the box approach' and his ability to take lessons learned in seemingly unrelated areas, and apply them to occupational hygiene, have inspired many modern hygienists, both in the UK and internationally, and I definitely count myself as one of them. There can be no doubt that through this book, Bob will influence many more and, in doing so, better protect the health of millions of workers.

It is generally agreed within the UK that although we have made some gains in health risk management over time, our success has not been as profound as that in managing safety risks. The key to solving this lies in the application of the basic principles of occupational hygiene, the preventative approach to occupational health. This book will go a long way to helping occupational safety and health (OSH) practitioners better understand these principles.

Starting out with the historical context, from Hippocrates, through Ramazzini, to the landmark Health and Safety at Work Act and the eventual birth of the COSHH regulations, the early sections of the book set the scene and explain the OSH landscape we see in the UK today. The book then moves on to the technical nuts and bolts of risk assessment, engineering control, and the role of PPE in controlling exposures. Although this will be familiar territory for many occupational hygienists and some OSH practitioners, it is clearly explained here in Bob's own unique style, blending well established (but still underused) guidance with case studies to maintain clear linkage to the workplace. These sections are packed with useful illustrations which highlight the good, the bad, and the ugly of real-world control solutions and are interspersed with thoughtful challenges to allow the reader to reflect on and consolidate the learning that is offered. These are followed by chapters on controlling skin exposures, a topic on which Bob worked extensively in his career, and the design and application of leading indicators of performance, which is thought provoking. But it was the closing chapters that really caught my attention. Here Bob covers the professional skills of decision making and inspiring others to secure buy-in. These topics can be overlooked when providing technical training, but these skills are absolutely essential if we are to create rounded OSH professionals who are able to communicate, influence, and educate others to achieve the ultimate goal of worker health protection.

A clear understanding of the knowledge and skills covered in this book cannot fail to better equip OSH practitioners with the right tools to control exposure to substances hazardous to health. In doing so, the book will improve standards of worker health protection for millions of workers, resulting in many, many more of them living healthy lives for longer, which has to be the aim of any practitioner in the field of OSH.

Chris Keen BSc (Hons) CMFOH COH

BOHS President 2022-23

From the President, Institution of Occupational Safety and Health (IOSH)

Great things are rarely achieved by one person, effective teams can achieve extraordinarily, but global teams really can change the world when they have a common goal. This book strives to achieve a common goal – Improving the efficiency and effectiveness of COSHH-risk management. We, as OSH practitioners, should support this common goal through our personal networks, and it takes just one conversation at a time.

Louise Hosking CMIOSH CEnvH

IOSH President 2021-2022

From the Chief Executive Officer, BOHS

Occupational hygiene" or a preventative approach to worker health protection is a term that has rather fallen out of fashion. In the '50s and '60s, there was widespread awareness of the contribution that a healthy working environment could make to public health and long-term sustainability.

The terms "occupational health" and "occupational hygiene" were used synonymously, to the extent that the last Parliamentary report on the subjects said that this is exactly what they should be. The decades since then may have seen a decline in the terminology and in the presence of "Occupational Hygiene Centres," which were a national network. However, the science of occupational hygiene has been kept alive and well by organisations like the British Occupational Hygiene Society and individuals like Bob Rajan.

Bob's book exemplifies the learning of decades and the interdisciplinary and multidisciplinary nature of the topic. For those who see occupational hygienists merely as measurement scientists, there will be a pleasant surprise. The discipline, often described as being a combination of science and art, brings together the science of the probable and the art of the possible.

This book exemplifies to the non-expert the range of techniques and technologies which allow us to manipulate the one truly human-constructed environment – the workplace – to be a place where humans can survive and thrive. By contrast, it exemplifies the true potential horror of our acceptance of the notion of "occupational hazards" when it comes to health.

I once had the pleasure of working on Lord Saatchi's team for the Medical Innovation Act. The by-line for this work was the question: "Can an Act of Parliament help cure cancer?" Parts of this book go beyond that to the simple and also subtle means by which occupational cancers can be prevented. But it's not just the life-threatening diseases, like cancers, that are tackled, but also the range of illnesses that haunt the lives of too many workers in our country.

Recounted in the inspiring and idiosyncratic style of a true polymath, Bob's book will open the eyes of the uninitiated and the expert alike to a very different perspective on the biggest social and economic questions of our time. As we struggle with the burdens of demand on our health service and the increasing pressures on social care for the disabled and those unwell in old age, we might ask how we can ever manage it. The answers lie in the pages of this book.

Sometimes quirky and perhaps subtly subversive, like the author himself, the book provides insights that show us that the workplace does not need to be a factory of pain and disease (as it still is for so many people in 21st-century Britain). It affirms that science, in all its facets, can throw armour around long-term human health. And when tempered with professionalism, human insight, and ultimately a sense that compassionate worker health protection can go hand in hand with commerce and innovation.

I'm delighted to commend this book to the widest possible readership.

Professor Kevin Bampton

Chief Executive Officer, BOHS

From the Chief Executive Officer, British Safety Industry Federation (BSIF)

Bob, congratulations on the completion of this valuable book. I believe it is an essential, informative tool that embraces the stakeholders throughout the chain and which will make a significant contribution to occupational safety and health in this country.

The effective execution of safety and health management is served by straightforward easy to understand solutions to everyday challenges, and this book is a must-have, easy-to-follow companion. Throughout the author's career, he has demonstrated a deep passion for safety and health and developed a wide range of tools to aid the communication of a range of messages. The author has played a key role in getting information to those that needed it. From a BSIF perspective, Bob Rajan has initiated and facilitated key campaigns such as "It's in your Hands" dealing with skin health, "Clean Air Take Care" covering RPE and its use, and of course, he was a key driver of the Fit2Fit competency scheme for face fitting of tight-fitting masks.

Throughout his career, his straightforward approach to communicating and amplifying key OSH messages has made people safer and healthier. This book is a terrific addition to the body of work from his career.

Alan Murray

Chief Executive Officer, BSIF

From the Acting Head of the Field Operations Division Health Unit, Health and Safety Executive (HSE)

I had the pleasure of working with Bob Rajan at HSE for more than a decade. He is a senior and well-respected professional, but in many ways, he is so much more than that. Bob is a proven thought leader whose drive and infectious enthusiasm are evident in everything he puts his mind to. He is often ahead of his time with his ideas, and the rest of us often struggle to keep up!

Bob has never been afraid to try new approaches to deal with old problems and often looked to other disciplines or sought out novel technologies and approaches to understand the barriers to change, and the drivers needed to overcome them. He has then skillfully applied these techniques to the practice of occupational hygiene in order to effect change.

Personally, I have no doubt that Bob has contributed significantly toward the reduction of ill health in the workplaces of Great Britain. Congratulations on your book publication.

Duncan Smith CFFOH FRSPH

Acting Head of the Field Operations Division Health Unit, HSE

From the Chief Operating Officer, National Examination Board in Occupational Safety and Health (NEBOSH)

Bob conveys the importance of COSHH-risk management with a clear passion and accessible writing style that delivers to a wide audience. There is a wealth of information, advice, and guidance that will enhance the practitioners' tool kit and will certainly be instrumental in winning hearts and minds. We are truly stronger together, and Bob's generosity in sharing his knowledge and experience knows no bounds!

Dee Arp Dip2OSH CMIOSH MIIRSM MCIEA

Chief Operating Officer, NEBOSH

From the Chair, Safety Groups UK (SGUK)

Safety Groups UK is the umbrella organisation for circa 70 occupational safety groups throughout the UK. These groups are run on a voluntary basis, providing a network for many like-minded individuals and organizations. As such, SGUK creates opportunities to support OSH initiatives and publications and then promote those widely.

This book, one of several in Bob's portfolio, follows a similar theme in getting various work-related health issues portrayed in laymen's language to make the content easily understood by all that read or refer to it. There is an abundance of practical examples, relevant photographs, and illustrations that make it interesting for any reader involved in or responsible for health risks at work, and it is not restricted to those directly involved in COSHH risk management.

The book reiterates the volunteering nature of SGUK, and the fact that electronic downloads are available is a bonus. Having been involved in the Safety Group movement for over 30 years and as Chair of SGUK, I would urge all OSH Practitioners and their employers to join a safety group close to them and benefit from the membership.

Norman Stevenson Dip SM Dip EM FIIRSM

Chairman, SGUK

From the Chief Executive Officer Royal Society for the Prevention of Accidents (RoSPA)

As a RoSPA Distinguished Service award holder, Dr Bob Rajan – Rajadurai Sithamparanadarajah OBE JP PhD has influenced an improvement in working conditions in the UK and the wider world throughout his working life.

This 'companion' will support RoSPA members, award winners and others to achieve effective exposure control within their organisations. It will help make sometimes complex issues easier to follow. The result of years of Bob's experience and endeavour will surely benefit many workers and their organisations'.

Errol Taylor CDir FIoD FRSPH
Chief Executive Officer, RoSPA

Chapter 1: Controlling Exposure to Hazardous Substances at Work

"A challenge does matter. It is only the first step to finding appropriate solutions."

1.1 Thoughts and work of Hippocrates and Ramazzini

As far back as 300 BC, **Hippocrates**[1], the father of medicine, **advocated the doctrine of airs, waters, and places**[2]. **He believed that the quality of these elements to which people are exposed were important to the health of individuals**[2,3]. Moving on, **the need to adequately control exposure to hazardous substances at work has been evolving from the time of Professor Ramazzini** (1633 to 1714), the father of occupational medicine. His curiosity led to investigations, involving a variety of occupations in foundries, tanneries and other workplaces, are captured in his book De Morbis Artificum Diatriba (Diseases of Workers)[3,4]. In this book, he discussed several work-related problems, including the health hazards of dust and metals; repetitive or violent bodily movements; and odd postures. **Ramazzini noted: preventing work-related ill health is better than curing it. He went on to propose that it is so much easier to foresee future harm and avoid it**[3,4,5]. Following his valued observations and advice hundreds of years ago, **isn't it distressing to see processes involving very toxic substances still being undertaken without adequate control?**

So, one of the lessons from his legendary work is: curiosity is an important attribute and a useful technique. It should be at the forefront of every OSH practitioner's mind when involved in RM activities. Curiosity, supported by competency, good interaction and communication skills, should help active engagement with people at work for implementing effective RM measures.

1.2 Developments in Great Britain (GB)

In Britain, improvements to workplace conditions and the need for adequately controlling exposure to hazardous substances and the associated ill health evolved slowly. During the 1800s, employers did not pay sufficient attention to worker health and safety[6,7,8]. It meant there was – (to a much-reduced extent, now too[9]) - inordinate disruption to life, deprivation, disease and death (4Ds)[10] among the exposed population, including young children who were used as cheap economic sources of labour[9,10.] To minimise the unacceptable effects of the 4Ds, the first

Factory Inspectors, with limited powers, were appointed under the provisions of the Factories Act 1833[6].

The Factory and Workshop Act 1878[11] empowered inspectors, whenever they saw fit, to require mechanical ventilation in workrooms in which dust, gas, vapour or other impurities were generated. In 1907, the 'Home Office committee on ventilation of factories and workshops'[12] not only produced recommendations on designing and using local exhaust ventilation (LEV) for controlling contaminants in workplaces, they also described some of the basic errors involved in ventilation design. Sadly, some of which are still seen in the workplaces of the 2020s. So, another one of the important challenges for every OSH practitioner involved with COSHH-RM is to remedy this situation.

The Inspectorate of the 1930s established asbestos 'dust datum' of 'acceptable conditions' in spinning mills[13]. Since then, asbestos related regulations, their approved codes of practice (ACoPs) and guidance have been updated and improved several times to help stem the suffering and deaths caused by exposure to asbestos dust. We need to apply the learning points from the asbestos experience for managing exposure to hazardous substances like silica dust.

The Factories Act of 1937[14] required that all practicable measures shall be taken to protect the employed persons against inhalation of dust or fume or other impurity and to prevent its accumulating in any workroom; and where the nature of the process makes it practicable, exhaust appliances shall be provided and maintained. The Act had self-imposed limitations through legal qualifiers like 'against inhalation' and 'where the nature of the process makes it practicable.' The Factories Act 1961 had similar provisions.

Further scientific underpinning, development of instrumentation/control equipment and recommendations for adequate exposure control measures against hazardous substances have seen rapid and progressive changes during the past seventy years[11,13,15,16,17,18]. Since its foundation in 1953, the BOHS and its members have distinguished themselves as standard setters in work-health related exposure control and inventors of important new technology. These have enabled key advances in risk assessment, measurement and exposure control[13,15,16,17,18].

The foundation of the current OSH system (includes regulations, orders, rules, ACoPs and guidance) in GB was established by the Health and Safety at Work etc. Act 1974 (HSWA)[19]. "One simple but the enduring principle of the act - that those who create risk are best placed to control that risk, whether employers, employees, self-employed, subcontractors, designers or manufacturers/suppliers of articles or substances for use at work - has led to GB having one of the best combined health and safety records in the world"[20].

1.3 The Control of Substances Hazardous to Health (COSHH) Regulations

The COSHH regulations came into force on 1 October 1989[21], almost 110 years after the Factory and Workshop Act, 1878[11] and fifteen years after the landmark HSWA[19]. Since 1989, COSHH regulations and the associated ACoP[22] have been updated several times, giving improved guidance to the industry.

1.4 What is a substance hazardous to health (SHH)?

In simple terms, COSHH applies to almost all manufactured substances and preparations (mixtures of two or more substances)**, process generated substances** (e.g. silica dust, wood dust, flour dust and rubber dust), **and biological agents** that have the potential to cause harm to health if they are ingested, inhaled, or are absorbed by, or come into contact with, the skin, or other body membranes. The legal definition will follow Figures 1 and 2 and Tables 1 and 2 below.

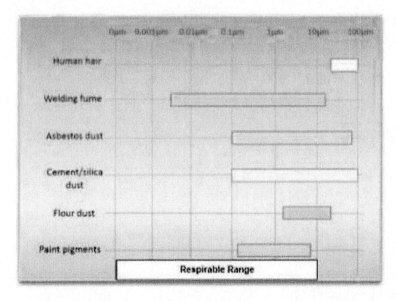

Figure 1[23] Particle size diameter ranges of example SHH in comparison with the diameter range of human hair, its average being 70 μm.

Inhalable particles, 100 μm and below, can enter the upper respiratory tract (nose, throat and trachea). **Respirable particles,** ranging from 10 μm and below, are small enough to be breathed into the lungs. Much of it can reach the air sacs (alveoli) of the lungs and can build up to cause lung damage. More details can be seen in Table 1.

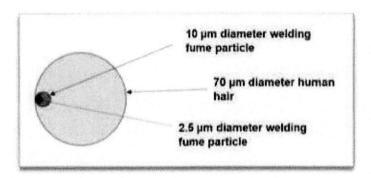

Figure 2 In this illustration, particle sizes (cross sectional diameters) are magnified several thousands of times - assuming uniform shapes - to make them visible for comparative purposes.

OSHKE

With reference to Figure 2:

1. How many 10 μm diameter welding fume particles can sit side-by-side on a 70 μm diameter human hair?

2. How many 2.5 μm diameter welding fume particles can sit side-by-side on a 70 μm diameter human hair?

3. How many 0.1 μm ultra-fine welding fume particles can sit side-by-side on a 70 μm diameter human hair?

So, lots of fine airborne particles can end up in lungs to cause problems.

A summary explanation of the properties of dust, fibres, mists, fumes, vapours and gases is discussed in Table 1, along with several visual demonstrations of fine particles in the air and how they can damage the lungs. A good understanding of this information is one of the keys needed for supporting COSHH-RM.

Table 1 Some properties of airborne forms of hazardous substances.

Airborne form	Description	Particle sizes	Visibility in air	Examples
Dust	Solid particles. (i) Can be supplied as products and used in activities like powder-handling, bread making, concrete making, rubber products making; (ii) Can be process generated, like stone dust and rubber dust.	**Inhalable particles,** 100 μm and below (*Human hair strand is about 70 μm in diameter*). **Respirable particles:** below 10 μm. Much of it can reach the deepest parts of the lungs to cause serious damage. Watch a 2-minute film on lung damage caused by silica dust: https://youtu.be/vCcON72KcMA	In normal room lighting: **Inhalable dust cloud** is partially visible. **Respirable dust cloud** is practically invisible below about 10 mg/m3. Watch a demonstration by Professor Fishwick using a teabag and a wood block. How does dust damage our lungs? - YouTube	Wood dust, grain dust, flour dust, silica dust. Watch: #LOcHERproject Greenbank High Case study - Lung diseases - YouTube
Fume	Vapourised solid that has condensed in the air.	In general, particle sizes range from 0.001 μm to 1 μm. https://youtu.be/zqnZGHdqWP8	Because of condensation (particles sticking together), fume clouds tend to be dense and are more visible than an equivalent amount of dust.	Fume generated by welding, rubber, soldering and diesel engine exhaust emissions.
Mist	Fine liquid particles process generated during activities like spraying, dispensing, and machining. They may be mixed with solids, such as in paints.	Particle size range from 0.01 μm to 100 μm. But the size range distribution can change as volatile liquids in the mist evaporate.	As for dust. Watch: https://youtu.be/7vdbZTomKPQ https://youtu.be/UYRNZI5e1Y8	Mists created by: Metalworking fluids, paint spraying, pesticide spraying, electroplating baths etc.
Fibre	Solid particles. The length of a fibre is several times bigger than its diameter, known as the aspect ratio.	Particle size range as per dust.	As for dust.	Asbestos, mineral wool, glass wool.
Vapour	Gaseous phase of a substance, which is liquid or solid at room temperature.	Behaves like gas or air.	Generally invisible.	Vapours of white spirit, petrol, toluene, iodine, and mercury.
Gas	A gas at room temperature.	Behaves like air.	Generally invisible, some coloured gases may be visible at high concentrations. (e.g. NO2)	Ammonia, chlorine, carbon monoxide.

Table 2[24] Globally harmonised health hazard symbols and their meanings.

Health hazard symbols	Meanings
	This pictogram with an exclamation mark represents substances that are harmful or irritating. The health effects associated are acute (effects are seen quickly), but they're less severe than something marked with the toxic symbol. H-statements in this category include those indicated below. For a comprehensive list, see GHS statements[24]. Hazard classes include: • Skin (H315, H316)), eye (H320), and/or respiratory tract irritants (H335) • Skin sensitisers (H317), which cause an allergic response, e.g. allergic contact dermatitis • The lowest level of acutely toxic chemicals • Materials with narcotic effects (drowsiness, lack of coordination, and dizziness)
	This pictogram, widely known as the toxic symbol, represents substances with the highest levels of acute toxicity. That means these chemicals have an immediate and severe (even lethal) effect on human health. For example, substances allocated H310, H311, H330, and H331.
	This pictogram is used for substances that present a health hazard over time (chronic). Hazard classes include: • Carcinogens, which cause cancer (H350) • Respiratory sensitisers (H334) • Agents with reproductive toxicity that affects fertility or in-utero development (H360) • Chemicals with target organ-related toxicity (H362) • Mutagenic chemicals that cause genetic defects (H341) • Substances with aspiration toxicity (H304)
	This pictogram represents substances that eat away at a material when they make contact. This symbol covers both physical and health hazards, for that reason, it shows both a hand and a surface. Hazard classes include those causing: • Skin corrosion or burns (H314) • Serious eye damage (H314, H318) • Corrosive to metals

COSHH[22] definition of substance hazardous to health (SHH), explained in coalface language, includes:

- Substances and preparations (mixtures of two or more substances) which are assigned "health hazard H-statement(s) and health hazard symbols (Table 2 above) under the globally harmonised classification scheme", enforced through the British Classification, Labelling and Packaging (CLP) regulations[24].

- The R-phrases scheme (now not in use), prescribed in the current COSHH ACoP[21] has five categories: harmful, irritant, toxic, very toxic and corrosive.

- Substances which have HSE-approved workplace exposure limits (WELs)[25]. Note: the threshold limit values (TLVs) set by the ACGIH® or the occupational exposure limits set by the European Union do not form part of the current WELs.

- Dust of any kind when present at a concentration in air (**dust trigger values**, see box below) equal to or greater than – (i) 10 mg/m3, as a time-weighted average (TWA) over an 8-hour period, of inhalable dust; or (ii) 4 mg/m3, as a TWA over an 8-hour period, of respirable dust. This will include process generated substances.

- A substance, because of its chemical or toxicological properties and the way it is used or is present at the workplace, creates a risk to health. This is a catch-all definition. Examples include process generated substances such as dust created by flour, foundry particles, stone and wood; welding fume and metalworking fluid mist.

- A biological agent.

Dust trigger values 10mg/m3 inhalable dust and 4 mg/m3 respirable dust. BOHS[26] and OSH experts[27,28,29] have concerns about these trigger values in COSHH regulations [21]. HSE recognises this:[30] 'there is a growing consensus in the occupational health and hygiene community that exposure to dust at levels below 10mg/m3 inhalable and 4mg/m3 respirable is a risk to the health of employees and other people affected by work activity. Therefore, it is important to ensure that any exposure to dust is kept <u>as low as possible</u>.' In the case of the term *as low as possible*, it would be prudent to take measures to reduce exposures as low as is reasonably practicable; and the COSHH principles of good practice (Section 1.8) must be applied.

1.5 Prevention, substitution and adequate control

The centrepiece of COSHH regulations is: always try to prevent exposure to SHH by taking preventive measures at the source. Example approaches for preventing the potential for exposure are listed below.

- Can you avoid using a SHH or use a safer process for preventing exposure, for example, using water-based rather than solvent-based products; or applying by brush rather than spraying?
- Can you substitute it for something safer, for example, swap a corrosive cleaning product for something milder; or use a vacuum cleaner rather than a broom for sweeping fine SHH dust?
- Can you use a safer form of SHH, for example, using a gel form rather than liquid to avoid splashes, a waxy or granular solid instead of a fine dry powder, e.g. using powered enzymes in an encapsulated granular form to minimise dust?

However, **it is not always reasonably practicable to prevent exposure to SHH during a process**, even when examples like those described above are in place. This eventuality is recognised, and requirements for exposure control are legislated in regulations 7(1) and 7(3). It means:

- Planning for, implementing and monitoring adequate control of exposure,
- Rectifying any shortcomings identified, and
- Being ready in case of an emergency.

OSHKE

It isn't always reasonably practicable to prevent exposure to SHH during a process. For example, when an encapsulated enzyme-based granular washing powder is automatically dispensed into cardboard containers for distribution and sale in shops. Think of potential exposure situations where fine powders could be created from formulated washing powders. *Examples: (i) During automated dispensing: vibrated dispenser (located between the bulk container and the discharge point into cardboard containers) may become blocked, requiring*

---

manual unblocking. This activity may require suitable respiratory protective equipment (RPE), even when a shadow vacuuming technique is used for minimising exposure to enzyme containing dust; (ii) During transport, storage and handling (various stages - at the factory, distribution centres, onboard lorries' and at supermarkets), the fine powder could be created by accidental spillages and grinding. These events will require attention and RM measures.

1.6 Measures to be taken for achieving adequate control of exposure

When considering measures for achieving adequate control of exposure, employers must (and OSH practitioners need to) consider and **apply protection measures appropriate to the activity and consistent with the risk assessment.** This kingpin legislative clause permits flexibility, innovation, initiative, proportionality, prudence etc. when applying the 'so far as is reasonably practicable' principle. The extent of its success is likely to be heavily dependent on the competency of those involved in the 'plan, do, check act' cycle.

Approaches to protection measures are:

- Replacing SHH or process which, under the conditions of its use, either eliminates or reduces the risk to the health of employees (regulation 7(2)). For example, using two-pack paints containing low boiling point isocyanate (a curing accelerator) for reducing the level of isocyanate vapour generation, in turn, helps to reduce inhalation exposure;

- Applying the hierarchy of controls measures in the priority order given and as appropriate to the activity and the findings of suitable and sufficient risk assessment - regulations 7(3);

- Applying measures such as limiting the exposure period, limiting the amount of SHH used at any one time, worker rotation, using general ventilation and providing welfare facilities - regulation 7(4);

- Reducing exposure so far as is reasonably practical, where exposure to carcinogens and mutagens are involved. Measures legislated in regulation 7(5) must be applied in addition to those in regulations 7(3) and 7(4).

However, **there appears to be a tendency to think rigidly and then promote and focus on the "hierarchy of controls" and compliance with WELs.** There are many practical reasons why this mode of thinking has limitations. They include:

- Practical controls are seldom of only one type but are mixtures of different strategies. This is foreseen in regulations 7(3) and 7(4). Recall the OSHKE example on granulated enzymes.

- There are only about 500 substances for which WELs[25] has been assigned. Many thousands of other SHH do not have WELs. So, when checking for adequate control, don't get hung up on those substances with WELs. Furthermore, just relying on compliance with WELs of substances on the day of sampling (in particular, using the results of one or a few air sampling measurements on the day for an individual operator or a group of workers performing similar tasks), will not meet the legislative requirements for adequate exposure control (Section 1.7), nor will it provide assurance that the controls were (and will remain) adequate.

- On the matter of WEL compliance and adequate control of exposure, BOHS[26] provides helpful, professional guidance to OSH practitioners and employers. They say, "The legal requirement to apply the principles of good control practice, as stated in the COSHH Regulations 2002 (and equivalent Northern Ireland legislation), is not widely appreciated by many employers. Consequently, some employers may not be complying with their legal duties to adequately control the exposure to substances hazardous to health, even if WELs have not been exceeded. The principles of good control practice include (amongst other things) the requirement to design and operate processes and activities to minimise emission, release and spread of SHH and this applies even if exposure monitoring has confirmed that the WEL (or dust trigger values) have not been exceeded." The sentiments of this advice are further supported by the joint report of BOHS and the Dutch Occupational Hygiene Society[31].

- For some SHH/processes, - such as diesel engine exhaust emissions (DEEE), foundry fume/dust, and organic solvents-based spray painting, - personal exposure monitoring for all the constituent substances with WELs can be resource intensive in terms of time and money required for engaging consultants, checking their credentials, paperwork, record keeping, reviewing information, communicating to operations, defending good control practice requirements when WELs are not exceeded etc. In the circumstances like these, resources committed for air sampling all the constituents are unlikely to provide effective contributions to productivity or adequate exposure control (see the previous bullet). A further discussion is provided in the box below.

DEEE may contain fine carbon particles (soot), nitrogen, water, carbon monoxide, carbon dioxide, aldehydes, oxides of nitrogen, oxides of sulphur, polycyclic aromatic hydrocarbons etc. HSE recommends that levels of carbon dioxide (a surrogate) above 1000 ppm 8-hour TWA in the workplace may indicate faultily, poorly maintained or inadequately designed control systems, in particular, LEV or roof extraction systems[32].

Molten metal foundry fume may contain dioxins, respirable crystalline silica, lead, mercury, nickel etc.

OSHKE: In this scenario, is it sensible, proportional and prudent to carry out TWA air sampling for all the constituent substances with WELs? *Here are some observations of HSE[33]: (i) "Employers used consultants for exposure monitoring. HSE does not consider some of the monitoring methods used as valid."; (ii) "Employers were using potentially unreliable data in their risk assessments"; (iii) "When commissioning exposure (air) monitoring, employers should request that inhalable foundry fume particles/dust using validated methods."*

Spraying two-pack paints containing isocyanate and six organic solvents (xylene, 1-methoxy-2-propanol and three isomers of trimethyl benzene).

OSHKE: If you decide to undertake air sampling to determine exposure levels, what substances will you monitor and why? *First, the relevant RA should include reasons why exposure monitoring is needed, as required by regulation 10 of COSHH. The RA might include reasons such as: (i) inhalation exposure to isocyanates can cause work related asthma, and there is a legal requirement to ensure exposure to isocyanates is reduced as low as is reasonably practicable; (ii) spray booth mist clearance time should be observed before lifting RPE visors to minimise exposure; (iii) by controlling the exposure to the serious hazard (isocyanates), the extent of exposure to solvent vapours could be kept under control; (iv) Three monthly biological monitoring (urine samples) will be used as an assurance. To note: The extent of exposure will be influenced by several exposure control modifiers. So, before any air or urine sampling is undertaken, an observation of leading indicators of exposure control effectiveness (design, use, checks and maintenance of control measures, work practices, adequacy of supervision,*

---

cleanliness, welfare facilities etc.), should be made to assess the situation to ensure that the principles of good practice are applied, and efforts are in place to maintain adequate control. Urine samples can help to understand exposure history for a period; A TWA air monitoring result is just like average speed pictures taken by speed cameras, nudging drivers to play by the rule within the monitoring window.

1.7 The test for adequate control of exposure

The requirements can be clearly seen by a closer examination of regulation 7(7). Control of exposure to a SHH shall only be treated as adequate if:

- The principles of good practice control set out in Schedule 2A is applied - 7(7)(a);
- Any HSE approved WEL is not exceeded - 7(7)(b); <u>and</u>
- The need to reduce exposure as low as is reasonably practicable has been met for a substance which carries the risk phrase R45 (H350), R46 (H340), R49 (H350), R42 (H334) or R42/43 (H334/H317) or for a substance or process which is listed in COSHH Schedule 1 or the 45 named substances listed in section C of HSE publication "Asthmagen?" - 7(7)(c).

In addition, employers must ensure that whoever provides advice on prevention or control of exposure is competent, as stipulated in regulation 7 of the MHSW Regulations[34] and regulation 12(4) of COSHH[22]. Experience and the **evidence presented in Chapter 2 and beyond will show that incompetent advice is a significant contributor to poor control practice.** So, you should always establish and be satisfied with the competency of people providing OSH support.

1.8 The "principles of good practice."

They are legislated in Schedule 2A of COSHH regulations[22] and are listed below.

a) Design and operate processes and activities to minimise the emission, release and spread of SHH.

(b) Take into account all relevant routes of exposure – inhalation, skin absorption and ingestion – when developing control measures.

(c) Control exposure by measures that are proportionate to the health risk.

(d) Choose the most effective and reliable control options which minimise the escape and spread of substances hazardous to health.

(e) Where adequate control of exposure cannot be achieved by other means, provide, in combination with other control measures, suitable personal protective equipment (PPE).

(f) Check and review regularly all elements of control measures for their continuing effectiveness.

(g) Inform and train all employees on the hazards and risks from the substances with which they work and the use of control measures developed to minimise the risks.

(h) Ensure that the introduction of control measures does not increase the overall risk to health and safety.

The principles overlap in their application and are not set out in rank order of priority. You should decide the order of application because many factors associated with SHH, process operations, organisation and individuals involved will influence the way the principles are applied for delivering and maintaining adequate (effective and reliable) exposure control measures. For example, the training requirement in item (g) will come before item (f) because the extent and methods of training will be influenced by the significance of the risk, operator experience/knowledge and the sophistication of exposure control measures to be used. Examples of good practice influencers include:

- The severity of the hazard presented by the SHH (e.g. irritant, corrosive, harmful, toxic or very toxic).
- Routes of exposure (e.g. inhalation, skin contact/absorption and ingestion).
- Exposure likelihood (e.g. unlikely, likely or most likely).
- The extent of exposure (e.g. high, medium or low).
- The duration of exposure (e.g. few minutes a day, occasional, daily).
- The extent of health risks associated with hazard/exposure (e.g. very serious, significant or minor)

- Individuals at risk (e.g. inexperienced workers).
- Quality and the type of control, its design, installation, use, tests, monitoring and maintenance.
- Competency and attitudes of those closely involved in the 'coalface' COSHH-RM cycle'.
- Methods used for communicating relevant information, e.g. signs, alarms, fail-to-safe devices, etc.
- The extent of supervision needed and applied.
- Quality/cleanliness of welfare facilities.
- Cleanliness of work areas.

As you will note, several **exposure modifiers play a part in achieving adequate exposure control,** and you will have to address these when helping and supporting operations or seek help from another competent person (CPs) such as a Chartered Occupational Hygienist.

1.9 Undertaking work involving SHH

COSHH demands that employers must not carry out work which can expose any of their employees to any SHH until:

- A suitable and sufficient assessment of the risks to employees' health created by that work is in place;
- The steps needed to comply with the regulations have been identified; and
- The steps identified have been put into operation.

OSHKE

1. Do the operations you support always comply with the three COSHH requirements described above?

2. In case of difficulties, how would you manage the situation? *This may be by providing adequate and suitable interim control solutions for the short term whilst urgent actions are taken to establish compliance. However, the approach taken will depend on the seriousness of the acute risks.*

3. What are your thoughts on the suggested approach described in item 2 above?

1.10 Controlling exposure to SHH so far, a brief summary

Over a period of about 33 years, up to 2022, the **COSHH regulations have energised vast improvements** in the ways SHH are used at work, **resulting in noticeable reductions in exposure levels**[35] and **work-related lung**[36] **and skin diseases**[37]. These trends are illustrated in Figures 3, 4, 5 and 6 below. In Figures 3, 4 and 5 make a note of the exponential reduction and plateauing. It is much harder to get things done when the conditions reach levelling.

However, there is no doubt that **improvements so far have saved many lives, improved the well-being of thousands of workers, reduced societal burden, and contributed to British economic wellbeing.** These improvements wouldn't have come about without the active involvement and contributions of many stakeholders (including 'coalface' OSH practitioners), effective implementation of adequate control measures and other positive actions like suitable training, labelling of hazardous products, safety data sheets and provision of good standard welfare facilities.

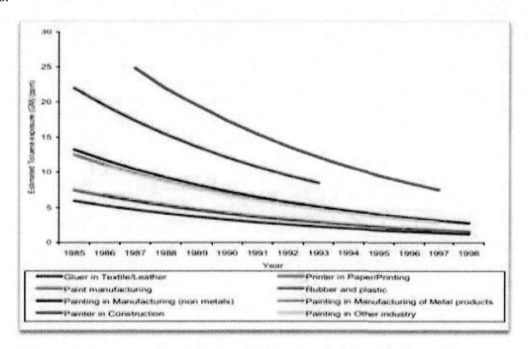

Figure 3[35] Estimated trends in toluene exposure by industries, using data from HSE inspection visits.

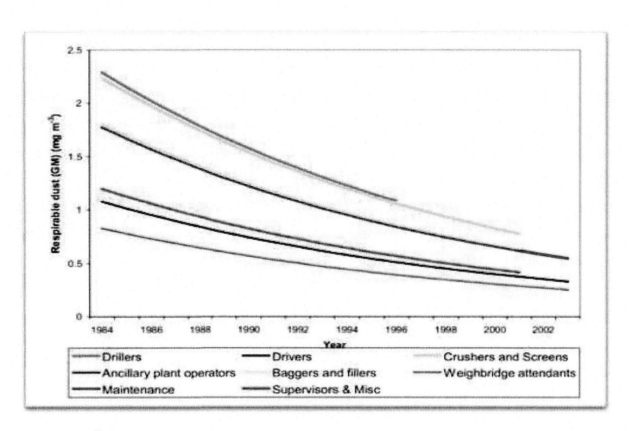

Figure4[35] Temporal trends in respirable dust exposure by occupation, using data from HSE inspection visits.

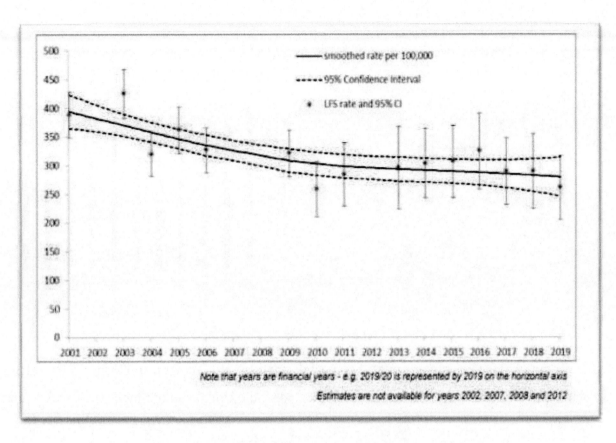

Figure 5[36] Self-reported work-related breathing or lung problems, in GB, for those who ever worked.

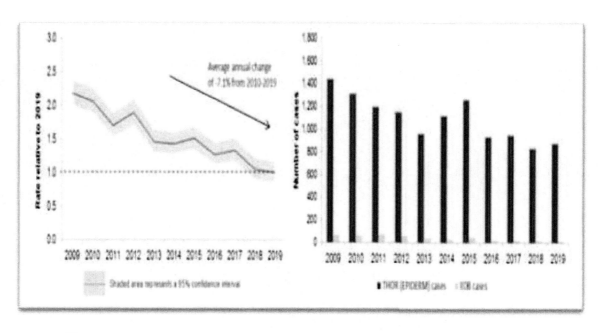

Figure 6[37] Trends in work-related contact dermatitis. (IIDB = Industrial Injuries Disablement Benefits; THOR/EPIDERM databases are operated by the University of Manchester, partly funded by HSE.

1.11 Proportionate work remains to further reduce the extent of exposure

Despite the vast improvements in SHH related exposure control and ill health reductions (Figures 3 to 6), a lot more proportionate and challenging work remains. One of the reasons is that the SHH related ill-health situation has remained relatively at a plateau in recent years, for example, the extent of work-related lung diseases (Figure 5), work-related asthma (Figure 7), and early deaths (Figure 8). It is important to note that although the rate of self-reported work-related ill health remained broadly flat since 2002 (Figure 9), in 2019/20 and 2020/21, it was above the trend observed, creating further concerns. Simply because the situation in Britain has reached a 'plateau' (Figures 3, 6, 7 and 9), employers (and OSH practitioners) cannot relax their exposure control efforts because legal obligations for ensuring adequate exposure control remain and everyone, at work, has the right for a healthy working life.

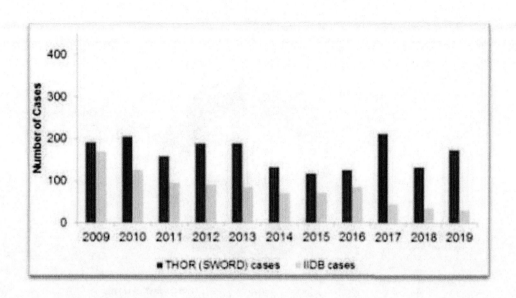

Figure 7[38] Estimated number of asthma cases reported by chest physicians and industrial injuries disablement benefit (IIDB).

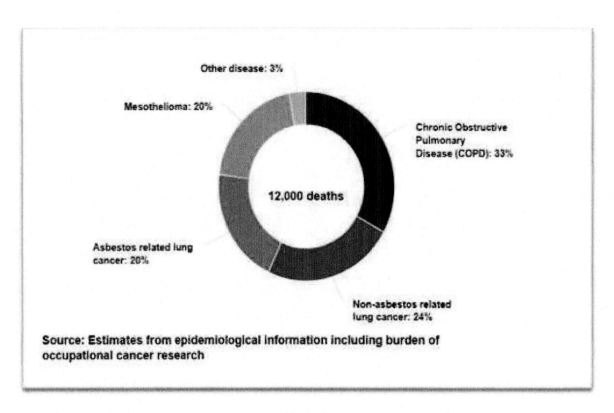

Figure 8[36] Occupational lung diseases contributing to estimated annual current deaths.

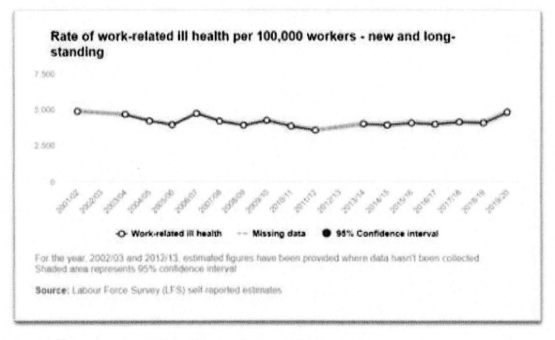

Figure 9[36] Work-related ill-health trends from 2001 to 2020.

At present, work caused cancers remain a great concern, which can be caused by prolonged exposure to chemical substances, or mixtures of substances, called carcinogens. These substances can be present in workplaces in many forms, such as solids, liquids, vapours, dust, fume, mists and gases. Exposure to these can take place by breathing in, skin absorption through the skin or swallowing (ingestion). Cancer starts when one or more cells in the body change abnormally due to exposure. It takes hold when the abnormal cells start to divide in an uncontrolled way but can potentially remain undetected for decades after harmful exposure. The UK's overall and work-related cancer statistics are shown below [39,40].

- Work-related cancers: ~18,000/year; Associated deaths: ~9,000/year
- All cancers: ~375,000/year; Associated deaths: ~166,000/year

Even though UK work-related cancer statistic[39] is about 20 times lower than all cancers recorded in the UK[40], there is no excuse for causing work-related diseases, including premature life-ending diseases like cancer to workers - as well as stress to workers, their families and strain to our National Health Service (NHS) - simply because they went to work.

1.12 Summary

The British OSH law[19] and society[41] demand that **all workers have the right to work in places where risks to their health and safety are properly controlled**. So, those who create OSH risks are best placed to control them, and law[19] places duties on them. OSH practitioners have professional duties to help and support employers in delivering better workplace health, like safety. As noted already, work-related ill health statistics have reached a 'plateau' but have been rising in recent years. This situation, especially inhalation related, demands curiosity, greater perseverance, innovation and focus for tackling avoidable exposure control failures and delivering a hammer blow to the current situation.

Chapter 2: Contexts for Helping to Deliver Good Control Practice

"For me, context is the key – from that comes the understanding of everything."
- *Kenneth Noland, American Artist.*

2.1 Introduction

Despite vast improvements in COSHH compliance, **hundreds of employers in GB** - with extensive support systems, such as HSE's help being available at the press of a few computer buttons - **have provided inadequate exposure control measures**. This statement is supported particularly by information in HSE's webpages, press releases, notice and prosecution databases[42,43], and visual images and discussions in this book. **On the other side** of the coin, Professor Löftstedt's independent review[44] on 'Reclaiming health and safety for all' noted that **"there is evidence to suggest that proportionate risk management can make good business sense."**

With these in mind, this Chapter explores OSH contexts which are positive as well as negative and suggests solutions for dealing with negative ones. Chapter 3 sets out some of the challenges and failures in COSHH-RM, and suggestions for tackling them are discussed. These are intended to help you deliver proportionate, prudent, effective and efficient COSHH-RM.

2.2 Exploring proportionate risk management

According to the Oxford Dictionary[45], **proportionality is the "principle that an action** (e.g. engineering control measures, using a broom to sweep dust, personal exposure measurements, and health surveillance), **a punishment etc.,** (e.g. an enforcement action by HSE, OSH related verbal warning to an employee), **should not be more severe than is necessary."** The UK Regulatory Committee[46] explains that **proportionality will always remain a matter of judgement** because it is neither possible nor desirable to set out exactly what a proportionate level of analysis is in all situations. It means that each case - for example, an OSH decision taken by a practitioner, an enforcement decision taken by an HSE inspector, or a sentencing handed out by a Court of law - should be judged on its own merits based on applicable transparent guidelines. In any case, personal biases and attitudes should be set aside. As a practical proposition, based on legal arguments and opinions[47], four interconnected tests could be used. My interpretation is explored below. The **Four distinct stages of proportionality tests are**[47]:

1. whether the **objective** (preventing an imminent danger to life, limb or property in the context of the HSW Act) of the **measure** (a Prohibition Notice (PN) issued by HSE) is sufficiently important to **justify the limitation** (a PN preventing the specified work, activity, or business activity being carried on at a worksite, until the danger is eliminated, prevented, or adequately controlled);

2. whether the measure and the justification for the limitation are rationally connected to that objective;

3. whether **a less intrusive measure** (e.g. an Improvement Notice (IN)) **could have been applied**; and

4. whether **a fair balance** (between the imminent danger and the continuation of the work, activity, or business presenting the imminent danger) has been **struck** between the **right of the individual** (the legal owner of the business) and the interest of the **community** (employees and/or public).

Note: In terms of COSHH, INs shouldn't be seen as less intrusive because, for health issues, they can potentially involve substantial expenditure depending on the extent of risk, the number of people affected, and the types of control measures needed. PNs focus on preventing serious personal risk from continuing, and INs are about securing compliance (re COSHH, generally through improved controls).

HSE report 'Reducing risks, protecting people'[48] **clarified proportionality** for OSH practitioners **as an action that is commensurate to the risks**. It is further clarified in HSE's enforcement policy statement[49], which includes:

*   Adopting a proportionate approach to enforcing the law *(for employers complying with the law)*,

*   Supporting businesses comply and grow *(you taking account of OSH-related and other expenditures for supporting the business comply and grow)*,

- Taking enforcement action *(employer taking OSH compliance actions)* which is proportionate to the OSH risks and to the seriousness of any breach of the law. This includes any actual or potential harm arising from any breach, the economic impact of the action taken, and

- Taking account of how far duty holders have *(your employer has)* fallen short of what the law requires and the extent of the risks created - (serious, significant or minor).

OSHKE

Does your OSH practice take account of the above on a routine basis and apply it during RM implementation?

The above said proportionality approach indicates that OSH practitioners should focus first on the most serious noncompliance, risks, and hazards. Thus, proportionate OSH delivery should be linked to transparency[50] and accountability[51] of decisions by CPs. Examples of proportionality-related issues are explored in Section 2.3. Now, **risk management** relates to activities required to:

- Identifying the hazard,
- Determining the likely level of exposure and the risk that can arise from it,
- Identifying the steps needed to prevent or control excessive exposure,
- Implementing the steps needed to prevent or adequately control the risk,
- Regularly checking and reviewing all elements of control measures for continuing effectiveness,
- Ensuring any shortfalls identified during checking and reviewing are rectified, and
- Taking account of other items discussed in this section

2.3. Examples of proportionality-related issues

The Löftstedt[44] review noted that COSHH-related costly administrative elements were:

- Risk assessment,
- Employee training, and
- Maintaining records of training.

These observations, made in 2011, are still experienced in 2022. The review also noted that in some cases, third parties, which include OSH practitioners, promote the generation of unnecessary paperwork and focus on OSH compliance activities that go above and beyond the regulatory requirements, so-called 'self-rule making' and 'gold plating'. The Risks and Regulation Advisory Council[52], in its report on OSH in small firms, noted that firms were keeping large numbers of reports on the recommendations of OSH consultants in case they may be taken to court. Lord Young[53], in his report to the government of the day, indicated that often unqualified OSH consultants have tried to eliminate all risks rather than apply the test in the Act[19] of 'reasonably practicable.

Sadly, similar findings were reaffirmed by HSE "insight" reports in 2019[54,55]. **It is important to note that third-party advice to duty holders can be compromised where a segment of the market delivers advice that is neither tailored to the user nor (in some cases) even competent**[54,55]. Other findings include:

- The role of businesses' compliance teams in driving requirements - "empire building."
- The "rules" community as having a role in compliance as a quasi-regulator. This community may include insurers, OSH consultants, buyers, those preparing specifications for tendering, and those selling accreditation, auditing systems, and other services and products.
- There are concerns that standards development (*which would include accreditation and OSH management-related standards*) is dominated by well-established, well-resourced companies and institutions, skewing the market to their interests, which may act as a barrier to innovation and smaller companies.
- Burdens on businesses have been made worse by OSH accreditation systems[56]. But **the law does not require accreditation**[57]. It is only one way of satisfying pre-qualification requirements when buying or supplying goods and services[56,57].

Accreditation (conformity assessment) impacts

- Accreditation schemes have at least some impact for 41% of SMEs, and a big impact for 19%

- Applied across many sectors - designed for construction, but biggest impact reported in education sector

- Overlapping accreditations – costing SMEs thousands per year. Barrier to growth?

- Impacts beyond health and safety? Schemes can include questions on: modern slavery, environmental management, money laundering...

"No real improvements to h&s management systems... no value in signing up to multiple schemes or refreshing each year. Commercial benefit only."

Figure 10[56] Impact of OSH <u>accreditation system</u> (accessed 5 May 2022).

Information in Figure 10 highlights the potential negative impacts of accreditation and exhibits over 50 British accrediting institutions! The insight reports[54,55] also noted that the Occupational Safety and Health Consultants Register (OSHCR)[58] is contributing in small ways to rectifying problems of the 'rules' community. However, the sentiments give a clue that the **OSHCR system requires significant improvements and robustness for identifying "specialism based" CPs.** So, when you are planning for, implementing, checking and reviewing the effectiveness of exposure control measures:

- Everything reasonably practical should be in place to keep out much of the criticism aimed at OSH practitioners and OSH in general. It includes challenging disproportionate and inaccurate advice or an inappropriate decision taken in the name of OSH and COSHH. As you well know, every profession has a small number of 'bad apples', so we need to self-police to get rid of those in OSH related professions. If you suspect that a service provider is incompetent in the area of service being provided, report to HSE and the relevant professional organisation.

- The 'rules' community and 'business compliance teams' should be challenged every inch of the way to prevent them from acting like a 'judge and jury', purporting to act in the best interest of employers', or injecting unwarranted fear factors without legally backed evidence. For example, advising employers to implement expensive/resource intensive management standards, data management systems, health surveillance, exposure monitoring and culture surveys in case of a claim or an enforcement action. Sometimes, just quoting part of COSHH or other OSH regulations without full legal context and value for money. In fact, you should demand that the 'rules' community should spell out (to employers) the shortcomings (if any) in implementing adequate control of exposure, including the eight principles of good practice. You should demand that their reports should be specific and concise on their observations, and any recommended action should be focussed entirely on compliance with minimum legal requirements, not on hypothetical claims. They should be asked to make conscious efforts to minimise the padding of their reports. I have seen copies of HSE guidance, books, unnecessary and superfluous sales literature and much more appended to OSH reports. Time is money, and padding causes distraction and a potential for a fat cheque. OSH practitioners should bear these in mind.

- When the 'rules' community or the 'business compliance teams' ask you to use recommendations in a product standard, checks should be made to ensure whether the requirements in the standard go beyond those recommended in relevant HSE guidance and proportionality.

- The 'rules' community/'business compliance teams' should be challenged when they use or recommend product/management standards without legally justifiable reasons.

- When selecting service providers, do not rely solely on the information in OSHCR[58]. Instead, seek evidence of competency.

In summary, "positive changes can be tough at the start; they can create enemies during the process, but are worth it at the end."

OSHKE

1. Why would an OSH practitioner keep paperwork that goes beyond the minimum legal requirements? *Is it to: increase workload; self-incriminate; or help HSE, prosecutors and insurance/ambulance 'chasers? Alternatively, is it to do with commercially available OSH accreditation/databases encouraging paper overload? Anything else?*

2. When you engage a person categorised as "rules" community/business compliance teams', do they encourage you to create and keep records that go beyond the minimum legal requirements?

3. Should the "rules" community be allowed to act like a quasi-regulator and create artificial requirements beyond the law and its compliance requirements?

4. Do you make clear to the "rules" community that when they offer their services to your employer (you), they should make it crystal clear that their advice and recommendations have taken account of the five decision making steps recommended in the 'Judge Over Your Shoulder'[59]. In summary, it would involve:

(i) **Where does the power come from to make decisions** – do I have the right competency; (ii) **Evidence gathering** - will I be acting with procedural fairness; (iii) **Taking decisions** - will I be taking necessary considerations on proportionality, prudence and seriousness of the risk and HSE/courts interests; (iv) **Notifying decisions** – giving reasons; and (v) **Responding to challenges** – from employers and OSH practitioners.

RM activities include looking out for opportunities for improving efficiency and effectiveness, productivity and RoI, as well as exposure (risk) control. These elements should act like 'hand in glove'. If you disagree, analyse the reasons, reflect and act accordingly.

On the positive side, from the time COSHH regulations came into force in October 1989[21], there has been a continuing advocacy by many OSH professionals for making the COSHH compliance process easy for effective implementation at the coalface. As a response to the continuing advocacy, HSE and many OSH professionals have been and are at the forefront of making the 'plan, do and check' part of the COSHH-RM cycle simple for small and medium-sized employers (SMEs), workers/managers/employers and OSH practitioners, examples include those described in references 26-30,32,33,60-72.

OSH practitioners know well that RM is like tightrope-walking. So, in every OSH-RM situation, it is the risk that is weighed (not the hazard, nor any individual word in legislation, ACoP or guidance) against the measures necessary to prevent or adequately control serious harm to employees and others. The greater the risk, no doubt, the more weight will be given to technology (including preventing design failures) and a lesser weight to cost, time and resources. This principle is enshrined in the Health and Safety at Work Act[19] as "so far as is reasonably practical." It is explained in simple terms by HSE[73]. Workplace application of the principle has been tested and interpreted by the British court of law[74]. In a health and safety prosecution, once it has been decided (for example, by an HSE inspector) that there has been an exposure to risk and the duty holder has failed to comply with the law, the employer may choose to prove that their actions were reasonably practicable, or they may just plead guilty; the court hearing the case will decide on the findings of facts, based on what has been presented by both parties. The principle has been put under the microscope[74-76], and so far, it remains the stalwart of the British OSH law.

2.4 Occupational health statistics

HSE regularly publishes work-related ill health statistics[77], some of which are pictorially shown in Figures 5 to 9 in Chapter 1. The 2020 report on occupational lung disease[36] indicates that each year around 17,000 workers report work-related breathing or lung problems. The same report tells us that, in 2020, there were in total 135,000 workers (past workers, now not in employment and those in work now) with breathing or lung related problems[36]. HSE's cost benefit analysis checklist[78] indicates that work-related lung disease is a serious burden to the British economy. Early deaths caused by work-related lung diseases stand at about 7,200 each year[36], excluding asbestos related deaths. If asbestos related deaths are included, the statistic will jump to about 12,000 deaths each year[36].

HSE's occupational health statistics are lagging indicators (after the events indicators, Figure 11). They provide useful information and support the drive for effective COSHH-RM. However, **it is prudent to check and understand the existing exposure control effectiveness at**

your own workplace. It can be done by enlisting the help of suitable leading indicators. The findings could be used to engage, explain and encourage operational colleagues to implement appropriate and adequate control measures where necessary. Chapter 8 provides help on leading indicators.

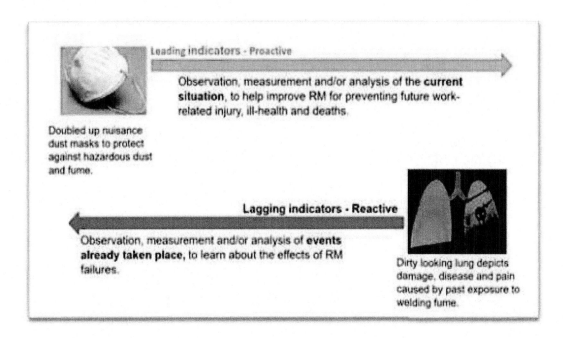

Figure 11 A brief explanation of the differences between leading and lagging indicators.

2.5 HSE and HM Courts activities

HSE conducts SHH related inspection campaigns[79-83], reinforced by appropriate enforcement actions[42] and prosecutions[43]. Since 2017, every year, about 200 COSHH related notices have been issued, many of them cite more than one contravention. These measures come about when, in HSE's consideration, employers failed to put in place adequate and suitable COSHH related exposure control measures to protect the health of their employees. Inspectors, in weighing up the quality of evidence available, will use their professional judgement about the nature of the exposure to risk. Where necessary, they seek advice and support from Specialist Inspectors, scientists, and relevant HSE Directorates[84]. Likewise, OSH practitioners/employers will be best served by using their professional judgement within their competency envelopes and, where necessary, seeking help from other relevant competent people.

Courts are imposing tougher sanctions when employers are found to be guilty of COSHH wrongdoing. For example:

- A company was fined £800,000 pounds with costs of £36,900 for causing work-related asthma[85]. In these types of cases, it is not about banning the hazard, e.g. metal working fluid or gloating on the big fine. It is about making the point that people with duties and responsibilities have failed to sensibly manage exposure risks arising from exposure to SHH, failed their shareholders and those people at risk. OSH practitioners can learn from the mistakes others have made and take appropriate actions to improve RM measures at their workplaces or in their consultancy work. With reference to this case, the prosecuting HSE Inspector said: "Companies need to make sure they consider workers' health just as much as their safety when carrying out risk assessments."

- A photo vending machine firm offering a 'take-your-own photo' service received a £100,000 fine with £30,000 costs for causing allergic contact dermatitis to two of their employees[86]. This sentencing may have led to accelerated RM measures for improving photo processing in vending machines - photos printed using sealed printing cartridges, a green chemistry approach - thereby helping to prevent transient and lone workers' exposure to chemicals and allergic reactions (see box below for more OSHKE explanation).

> **Green Chemistry**[87] is about reducing or eliminating the use or generation of (*exposure to*) SHH. It can be achieved during the design, manufacture, application and waste management of chemical products. It is not anti-industry or anti-profit. It is about curiosity-led innovation, initiative and/or implementation of approaches to protect the environment, workers and profitability by reducing waste and cost.
>
> **Photo firm case**[86]above: By using "green chemistry" for exposure prevention through design, the firm would have gained good medium to long-term RoI. The likely advantages would include reduction in: (i) packaging and storage costs; (ii) storage space requirements and the associated gains; (iii) shipping, transportation and waste management costs; (iv) paperwork associated with COSHH-RM; and (v) manual handling tasks for the transient and lone workers; as well as the elimination of in-situ wet-chemistry.

> **OSHKE:** on the photo firm incident, plausible questions. (i) Would you, day-after-day, manually mix and make buckets of working solutions of photo-processing chemicals from concentrates which are respiratory and skin sensitisers? (ii) Would you do the job on the worktops of handwashing stations in supermarket toilets? (iii) Would you manually carry the bucket with gurgling sensitising chemical solutions, supported by your tummy and unprotected hands? (iv) Would you expect your operatives to do these jobs? (v) How would you feel and react when the affected workers tell you that they cannot button their shirts because of the damage and pain caused to their skin by allergic reactions? (vi) What would you say to the OSH practitioner(s) who agreed (if they did agree) to the operational wet-chemistry related COSHH-RA and the associated RM implementation steps?

- A large manufacturer was fined £100,000 with £30,000 costs for causing occupational asthma to a soldering worker[88].

- An automotive engineering company was fined £100,000 after an employee had an allergic reaction at work[89].

- Two apprentices suffered chemical burns when cleaning the vehicle ramps in the workshop using a chemical from an unlabelled container. The company was fined £360,000 and ordered to pay costs of £12,622[90].

These are just a few examples to highlight the risks to employees from exposure to SHH. These serious avoidable injuries could have happened due to various competing factors, including incompetency and inattention. By consulting the cited references for the above examples, you will be able to get to know about the likely control failures, postulate why they may have happened and learn from them.

Many more examples can be found in references 42 and 43. In each of the cases, it is probable that companies' sustainability management analysis/profit and loss accounts would have taken account of relevant OSH-related actions and wasted costs. These may arise from: incompetency among OSH and operations personnel; HSE's fees for intervention; court fines; other penalties such as court costs and hikes in insurance premiums; loss of expertise where directors and others are barred from holding office; production delays; investigations; reports preparation; statements taking; and dealing with relevant stakeholders (lawyers, trade unions, press etc.). Example case studies cited in this section illustrate the need for OSH productivity improvements in all areas of the 'plan-do-check-act' cycle and to blend-in curiosity, proportionality, prudence and financial factors in COSHH-RM. Chapter 10 provides an introduction to inspiring OSH buy-in by operations.

2.6 Work-related lung diseases, HSE's priorities

According to HSE, **work activities** involving SHH that are **at "high" risk of causing lung problems** to include **cutting, drilling, sanding, welding, stonework, woodworking, baking, milling, quarry work, cement and concrete manufacture**[91]. If you provide OSH-RM contributions to any of these 'high-risk' activities, it is prudent to use HSE's COSHH Essentials task-specific direct advice sheets[92]. They provide an effective route for identifying the necessary control steps and doing COSHH-RAs. With relevant information in hand, you can engage CPs for designing, installing and maintaining the control steps and could use leading indicators to check the effectiveness of exposure controls.

Airborne forms of hazardous substances of serious concern are dust, fibres, mists, and fume[91]. OSH practitioners should take a keen interest in RM associated with these. However, you should keep in mind that ill health problems can also be caused by solvents and their vapours, gases, as well as microorganisms. For example, exposure to microorganisms found in metalworking fluids and cooling towers can cause serious harm. A summary explanation of dust, fibres, mists, fumes, vapours and gases can be found in Table 1.

The main types of work-related ill-health arising **from "excessive exposure" to SHH health are asthma, chronic obstructive pulmonary disease (COPD) and lung cancer**[91]. Other work-related ill-health problems include lung infections, dermatitis, skin cancers, and liver and kidney diseases. A further explanation of "excessive exposure" is provided in Section 4.6.

2.7 Needs of SMEs and the frontline

Small firms want simple tools that describe what they must do in plain language[54,55,93]. However, any practical tools developed, such as the COSHH Essentials Control Banding (CB) of SHH[94], should have sound scientific and technological basis[93, 95-100]. Practical electronic books, like this one, summarising information contained in thousands of pages of HSE/other publications and web pages, are useful because more and more OSH practitioners and firms are using the internet to access information and help. OSH **presentations, training, reports and guidance** on exposure control solutions **should consider** a significant increase in **pictorial, diagrammatic and practical content**[101-104]. When including pictures, you should ensure that they are as diverse and inclusive as possible. Also, where practical:

- Use real-world images rather than abstract ones.
- Use a range of media to improve the effectiveness of communication, for example, posters[105], games[106], short but effective films[107], and practical demonstrations[108].
- Present only one key point in a sentence.
- Aim to include fewer acronyms.
- Avoid acronyms which are hard to remember and difficult to interpret.
- Limit abbreviations which are not widely known and used in OSH circles and/or among operatives unless they serve a useful purpose in communication.
- Avoid jargon common to OSH practitioners and specialists, especially when communicating with operatives.
- Use analogies and metaphors with great sensitivity. Use them only where it is appropriate and relevant for explaining issues. The purpose should be to gain interest, attention, trust, and action and to help the recall the information by your audience.

An HSE survey in 2018[110], (30 years after the implementation of COSHH regulations) found that employers, employees and OSH practitioners felt that the regulations provide a useful framework for setting up organisational policies and processes for managing the risks from SHH. However, **managers and employees want support with translating regulatory requirements at an operational level ("coalface"). This call for help covers** the full scope of the regulations, **from knowing how to conduct risk assessments to ensure the effective implementation, maintenance and monitoring of controls.**

Respondents to the survey also said that they wanted greater clarity about what they needed to do to comply with COSHH regulations. **They considered that simplifying the regulations and** the supporting guidance, as well as standardising tools and information sources, will help to support compliance. These findings reflect those reported in the early years of 2000[93, 101-103,109]. This book takes account of these findings, and the examples and ideas discussed in this book should support your RM efforts.

2.8 Summary

The context, as discussed, tells us that OSH practitioners and other stakeholders have lots more work to do. In fact, injecting curiosity, simplicity, proportionality, prudence and productivity into COSHH-RM activities would lead to significant positive changes. In addition, OSH practitioners should increase their focus on:

- **Ensuring that hazards, risks and control measures are communicated effectively for impact and action.** (The meaning of 'effectiveness' is explored in Chapter 9);

- **Competently helping and ensuring that adequate and suitable exposure control measures are in place.** They should comply with COSHH-eight 'principles of good practice', proportional to risks being mitigated, as well as practical for the operatives to use them; and

- **Checking and reviewing are done proportionately and effectively to ensure control measures are used correctly and maintained properly.** Leading indicators are discussed in Chapter 8.

Chapter 3: Challenges and Failures

"The challenge is to stay cool enough to handle the pressure in the moment so that you can succeed in the future."

- *Jurgen Klopp, Football player and manager.*

3.1 Introduction

In general, OSH practitioners face many technical, financial, communication, engagement, and organisational challenges when attempting to instigate and help operations to implement adequate and suitable RM measures[111]. Since the implementation of the COSHH regulations in 1989, **there have been many challenges and failures in achieving adequate control in many workplaces**. In this chapter, several examples are listed with potential solutions so that you can reflect on these issues and take responsive actions, where appropriate.

3.2 Long latency and work-related ill health

Work-related long latency (chronic) **ill health cases aren't instantly graphic, visual and immediately impacting like safety-related incidences.** Traditionally, health issues in workplaces have been and still seem to be, harder to tackle than safety issues. This is reflected by the British statistics on work-related fatalities (~120/year)[112] and deaths caused by excessive exposure to SHH (~12000/year)[113]. Some underlying reasons could be:

- Safety has matured at a greater pace since the implementation of the HSW Act in 1974.
- Many coalface OSH practitioners may be highly conversant on safety-RM rather than on Health/COSHH-RM.
- After a safety-related event, the need for preventing future injuries, fatalities and/or damage to property and equipment is immediately obvious to OSH practitioners, duty and purse holders.
- The cause and effects of work-related ill health are often not clearly linked. While some cases of ill health are clearly related to work activity, such as exposure to isocyanates, lead, benzene and asbestos, for many SHH, the cause may be less clear. However, **health hazards pictograms, health related H-statements and their meanings** (Table 2, Chapter 1) **are designed to be helpful to employers, OSH practitioners and operatives.**

- Many serious occupational diseases are associated with a long period of 'latency', some up to 30 years, between exposure and development of ill health, making the links even more difficult to establish. This also means that after recognising the problem and making changes in working practices to reduce exposure, there may be a long delay before a reduction in the causes of ill health and death is seen, as with asbestos and silica dust.

As a productive way for facing these SHH related RM conundrums, HSE led campaigns often focus on serious exposure/ill health control challenges (Section 2.6). Paying attention to these SHH and the associated activities and acting on HSE's exposure control recommendations will make sense because:

- HSE recommendations should make it easier for you to explain the requirements to your operations colleagues.
- HSE would have produced task specific direct advice sheets[92] giving details on control steps for carrying out RAs and implementing RM measures.
- There can be potential opportunities for reducing expenditure on consultants who provide RA, exposure monitoring, training and record keeping services. COSHH task specific sheets/guidance, HSE's RA template (Section 4.16) and leading indicators of exposure control effectiveness (Chapter 8) would make these matters easier.
- You may be able to control the expenditure on health surveillance. To start with, ensure (i) your RA is adequate and suitable; (ii) COSHH principles of good practice are in place; and (iii) collect information on control effectiveness to support the adequate implementation of the good practice. Then decide whether health surveillance is appropriate, as required by law[114]. HSE guidance[114] on health surveillance can be a little daunting to read and difficult to obtain practical guidance, including on matters like the need for keeping records for 40 years, HSE's experience on this over 50 years and its cost benefit analysis. Based on the 'to start with' three items described above, if you cannot decide whether 'health surveillance is appropriate for the protection of the health of those at risk' (COSHH regulation 11), as a responsible person, and to protect your employer and yourself, in the first instance you will have to take action to address those three items and then use a suitable health check questionnaire. For those at risk of

occupational asthma caused by exposure to SHH, use HSE's Health questionnaire[115]. Alternatively, consider using the - University of Cambridge[116] template. For those at risk of occupation-related skin problems, consider using one of the following: (i) skin surveillance questionnaire[117], (ii) skin surveillance questionnaire-nhs[118] or (iii) questionnaire by the University of Cambridge[116]. You may use the questionnaire approach before engaging health consultants, potentially saving a considerable amount of money, paperwork, and time and for minimising the time workers are away from work to see health consultants.

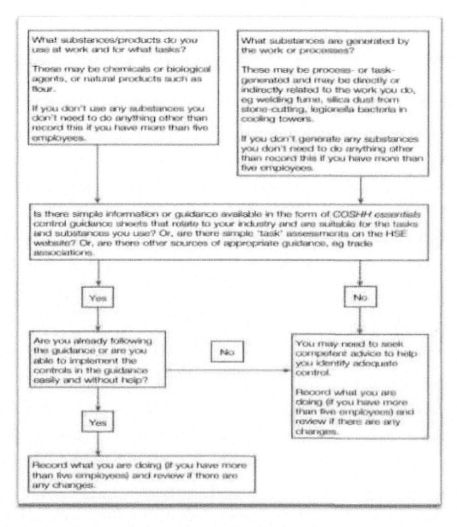

Figure **12**[22] A route map towards adequate control.

This Figure shows the COSHH ACoP recommended route map for assessing adequate exposure control. Contents of this Figure may be used for a simple brainstorming inquisitive cross examination to establish whether the employer (you) has succeeded in their effort/duty towards adequate control.

Based on Figure 12, you may create 'open' questions in your thought process. Here are five examples: (i) At work, do I use hazardous products/substances to health? (ii) Do I know the tasks in which these SHH are used? (iii) Do the people involved in delivering adequate control have the required competency to do their job? (iv) Are the control measures recommended in COSHH-Essentials direct advice sheets being followed? (v) Are we using suitable leading indicators to check exposure control effectiveness?

Furthermore, questions based on the contents of Figure 12, along with work activities relevant to the operatives who are being trained, could be used in training and risk awareness sessions. As a rule, "No" or any other answer other than yes, would suggest complacency, lack of awareness, control failures, and/or incompetency.

3.3 Risk sharing and transfer

There is a real potential for Ill health risk sharing and **risk transfer** between employers as well as through insurance underwriting. During their working lives, employees may work for several employers. Exposures resulting in chronic ill health may have occurred in more than one workplace, resulting in risk-sharing. The legally required employer liability insurance is a risk transfer mechanism. It shifts the responsibility of potentially unfavourable outcomes against any financial risks from the employer to the insurer, for example, on COSHH-related ill health, sickness absence, early retirements and civil claims. There are other ways, too, including sales contracts, employing third parties, and providing information in safety data sheets and user instructions on SHH.

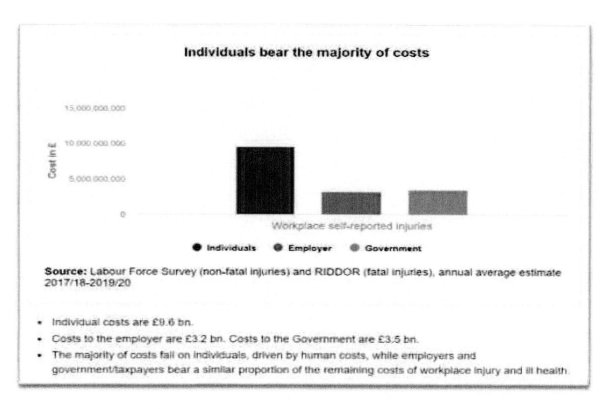

Figure 13[119] Cost of workplace self-reported injuries.

The consequences of risk sharing and transfer are indicated in Figure 13. It shows, at present, a large proportion of the cost burden of work-related ill health falls, in the main, to individuals and public funding[119]. Public funding includes disability benefits, NHS, tax-payer funded legal and other support and enforcement services such as HSE. It means employers, who fail to adequately manage COSHH exposure control requirements, could pass on a significant burden to individuals, public services and the government, as shown in Figure 13. This goes against the fundamental requirement of the GB OSH system – those who create risks are best placed to manage them. OSH practitioners can and should help to shift the balance.

Because of the risks-sharing and risk transfer potentials, it is possible that some employers may not pay sufficient attention to implementing adequate and suitable COSHH controls measures. These may include prevention of exposure and ensuring control measures are designed or selected, installed, used and maintained by CPs[120]. These problems may have an impact on what OSH practitioners do to help manage risks arising from exposure to SHH. In these cases, your five senses led curiosity would give you a good indication of how best to deploy your competency and professional effort. **You may demonstrate the extent to which an employer's organisation is**

compassionate, considerate and compliance delivering. This approach could stir-up their thought process for positive action. An example self-assessment approach developed by the <u>Scottish Healthy Working Lives</u>[121] could be used to a good effect. Using this approach could help to minimise the costs of employing RA consultants to assess the suitability of your current OSH policy, develop a new policy; auditors to undertake OSH culture surveys; consultants to undertake OHS management protocols development and assessments based on ISO 45001[122], and keeping large numbers of reports and information in expensive OSH databases. Money and time saved could be redeployed for delivering sensible and cost-effective RM to comply with the minimum requirements of the law.

3.4 Self-employed and COSHH

Many workers across a variety of industries are self-employed[123] and often perform transient, peripatetic and/or lone working[124]. These can present many OSH challenges, such as a lack of suitable training and OSH-RM competency. **However**, in recent years **there has been an appreciable shift among the self-employed to look after their OSH at work. OSH practitioners should keenly support this shift** by providing positive nudges, as in safety. For example, when contractors submit tenders to do work for your organisation, always insist and demand competency, not a certificate of accreditation. According to HSE, accreditation does not drive real improvements in OSH[54,55,56,] and the law does not require accreditation[57]. Whereas accreditation logos may help companies to produce sales and marketing adverts. If you happen to insist on accreditation, you will have to seek accreditation information from potential contractors, check and validate the information provided, keep records, maintain paper mountain etc. These can drive-up OSH and productivity costs, eat into RoI, may make your job harder and divert your efforts away from compliance and competency requirements.

3.5 Extent of COSHH awareness

In 2019, a survey of companies indicated that **only 54% of companies have some level of awareness of COSHH requirements**[125]. This finding, as it stands after nearly thirty years of COSHH, should be a serious concern for many OSH stakeholders. An earlier survey by HSE in 2005 (nearly 17 years after the implementation of the COSHH regulations) found that 35% of SMEs had not heard of COSHH[126]. So, a significant lack of COSHH awareness among employers and employees is a serious challenge and can be a severe impediment to making progress, including among transient workers. However, a variety of HSE initiatives, many of which were widely discussed on social media platforms, should go a long way to improving awareness and supporting your efforts in delivering exposure control effectiveness. OSH practitioners should maximise the effective use of the internet, social media, and virtual and visual technologies for helping to deliver effective COSHH-RM.

3.6 Potential scarcity of competent designers

An apparent scarcity of competent LEV designers could present a challenge and concern to coalface OSH practitioners and for effective COSHH-RM. A cursory web search (October 2021), using search terms 'COSHH and air monitoring' and 'COSHH and LEV testing', provided a listing of several commercial sources offering help in these areas. When using the search terms "COSHH and exposure control suppliers", "COSHH and engineering control suppliers", and "COSHH and LEV suppliers", there were few commercial sources listed as offering the design of extraction systems or LEV. Always remember a consultant's competency in LEV testing does not make them competent in designing and installing LEV. Taking these into account, always seek confirmation from your LEV design consultant that they have, as a minimum, (i) successfully completed a relevant BOHS course on basic design principles of LEV or an equivalent, (ii) can provide evidence of their design competency, and (iii) have successfully designed other control projects and can provide evidence. You can use their evidence to compare against examples of pitfalls described in this book and in HSE's guidance on LEV[127]. By avoiding these pitfalls, you will gain control over the effectiveness and costs that may arise from noncompliance.

3.7 OSH Admin failures

Many COSHH risk assessments have failed to document exactly **what suitable and adequate exposure control steps are needed or how they will be implemented before starting work**[42,43,120]. **Employers have also failed to implement control steps identified** in COSHH risk assessments[42,43,120]. To minimise RA-related failures on high concern activities (section 2.6), seek help from HSE's task related direct advice sheets[92].

3.8 Designing exposure controls and consultation with operatives

In many situations, exposure control solutions may be designed and provided without any consultation and involvement of operatives who will use them. A report by RoSPA[128] noted that the extent of worker involvement in OSH in non-unionised participant organisations is determined in part by various factors, including organisation size, sector, history, location, culture and the willingness to invest money and resources. This is an unsatisfactory situation, and in any event, the law requires that employees or their representatives must be consulted on matters of OSH[129]. HSE provides a summary of potential advantages of consultation[129]. As I have not identified any prosecutions on this matter[43], here are some nudges for you to consider. Do you always involve operatives and take account of their suggestions and inputs when:

- Undertaking and agreeing to COSHH-RAs, which will include control steps, the need or otherwise for exposure monitoring and health surveillance?
- Conceptualising and designing (or buying) adequate and practical control measures?
- Installing and implementing control measures?
- Designing and delivering training and risk communication?

OSHKE

Consultation with employees is better than spending money on culture and ISO 45001 surveys. Your thoughts.

3.9 'Unworried'/unaware workers

As you know, many serious occupational diseases are associated with a long period of 'latency'. Because of the long latency associated with SHH exposures, some workers may be 'unworried' or unaware of the need for adequate exposure control measures.

In Figure 14, the top lefthand picture shows a workplace where there was a potential for skin exposure to and skin absorption of a carcinogenic substance. Work equipment and other work surfaces are contaminated with the yellowish-looking substance (positive: control panels are covered with polythene). The top right picture shows a worker being exposed to silica dust (not under control with at-tool extraction or a partially enclosing extraction both). The bottom picture shows a worker who suffered allergic contact dermatitis caused by exposure to a sensitiser.

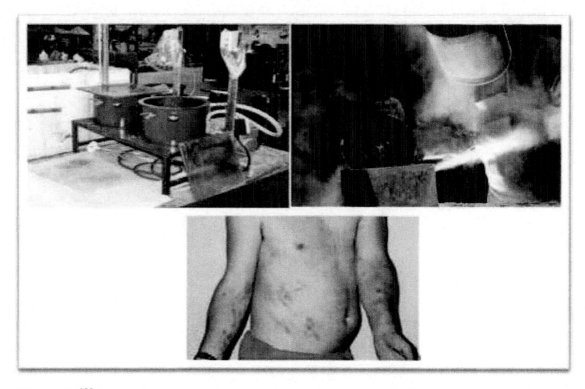

Figure 14[130] Example situations where a question on unworried/unaware workers issues may be raised.

OSHKE

Figure 14 above shows three work-related exposure scenarios.

1.   As they stand, do you consider that in any of the situations shown, employers would have played a responsible role in implementing good control practices? *No, not satisfactorily or highly unlikely.*

2.   Do you consider that the operatives involved could be considered 'unworried/unaware' workers? *This is only a possibility, nothing more. Others include: employees may not raise concerns, fearing that they may lose their jobs; it could be associated with 'It's part of my job' attitudes/believes; OSH practitioners involved may lack competency and/or influence on selling OSH to operations. Any more?*

3.   Do you come across situations like these in your workplace? *You decide. In many work situations, exposure control shortcomings could be better managed by suitable plan-do-check-act RM, including consultation and involvement of operatives and using positive risk communication and nudging techniques (Chapter 11).*

3.10 Blaming employees for control failures

Anecdotal evidence suggests that there appears to be a perception among some employers and a small number of OSH practitioners that 'employee noncompliance makes it harder to implement adequate exposure control.' It should be noted that managing "human errors/behaviours" becomes a reality only when we include employers, consultants, designers, supervisors, managers, site-based trade unions personnel and OSH practitioners along with employees. This interrelated reality is powerfully and visually expressed in Figure 15 below.

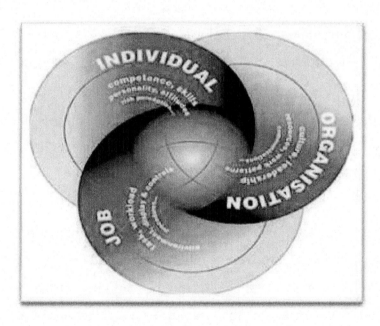

Figure 15[131] Human, job and organisation factors in OSH-RM.

When employers fail in their duty to provide suitable practical control measures, or consult, train and supervise employees, it is no good to blame employees for exposure control failures. It is just an easy option and a distraction. HSE is clear on human error management: *"It is quite wrong to believe that telling people to take more care is the answer to these problems."* [131]

Figure 16[130] Incorrect use of gloves, the glove was used inside out.

A simple example in Figure 16 illustrates the importance of integrating technology, administration, people involvement and good interactions for achieving and maintaining adequate control. This Figure shows evidence of the incorrect use of gloves. From the employer's side of the bargain, the likely failure factors that could have contributed to this incorrect use include failure:

- To provide suitable at-source control measures to avoid skin contact.

- To consider alternative ways for providing a suitable safe working distance (SWD)[22].

- To consult operatives before recommending the use of gloves.

- To inform operatives about the health risks associated with dermal exposure to solvents and dyes.

- To train operatives on correct donning, doffing, use, replacement and storage of gloves.

- To provide adequate support and supervision.

OSHKE

1.	Almost all safety related OSH practitioners: (i) will be aware of safe working load (SWL) requirements when dealing with lifting, loading and load anchoring equipment; (ii) will ensure the equipment of the kind described in (i) are marked with SWL, and the marking is visible on the relevant equipment and elsewhere; (iii) will make sure the equipment are regularly tested for integrity; and (iv) will insist that operational activities performed within SWL limits to prevent incidents/accidents/fatalities.

2.	Are you aware of the safe working distance (SWD) requirements in COSHH-ACoP?

3.	If yes, do you put the requirement into action in COSHH RAs, RM and explain/demonstrate in training?

Moving on, an industrial relations agreement led to operatives being paid an additional amount of money (known as "danger money") to their hourly rate for wearing half-mask RPE when working with a highly hazardous fibrous substance[132]. The site-based industrial relations agreement tried hard to block the work from being moved to a new facility with suitably designed exposure control measures because of the fear that the operatives would lose their entitlement for the "danger money". In this case, operatives were caught in the middle and were subjected to a negative nudge – "danger money". Occupational hygiene professionals used various approaches to win hearts and minds, including a calculated risk-taking - invited HSE inspectors and Specialists to assess the new facility and the effectiveness of control measures provided in the facility. Workers were paid a bonus for participating in the research. A positive assessment outcome, based on an independent expert evaluation, helped to win arguments. There are many situations like this where employees are subjected to negative nudges, potentially leading to short-term gain and long-term pain.

OSHKE

1.   How do you help implement the legal requirements to consult employees on matters of OSH?

2.   How do you inspire OSH buy-in among operations colleagues? *An introduction is provided in Chapter 10.*

3.11 OSH consultants' points of view

Some OSH consultants may express the view that exposure controls fail when there aren't adequate company policies, processes or sophisticated documentation systems. Many of us will agree that simple, usable and manageable admin systems form part of OSH-RM. However, even if you have all these operated by high-level, sophisticated administrative systems, 'HSE legal posters', and sophisticated COSHH data recording systems, no good will come if they aren't actively supported by adequate and suitable training, instruction, supervision, leadership[133,134] and effective exposure control measures at the source. A cursory review of the HSE prosecution database[43] would show Financial Times Stock Exchange (FTSE) listed companies - potentially employing highly qualified professionals, including OSH practitioners and using high-level policies and procedures - ending up in Courts of law for failing to provide and maintain adequate exposure control, sometimes failing to implement basic common-sense controls such as correctly labelling a storage container (a precursor led to serious health related injuries).

3.12 Consultants and suppliers and their advice

HSE's high level strategy on occupational lung disease[135] recommends that **there is a need to improve the way consultants and product suppliers give advice to employers, ensuring that it is fit for purpose.** OSH practitioners should respond positively to observations such as "consultants can provide advice that is not required by law and delivers little or no benefit to workplace OSH, only adding further burdens to businesses[44,52-56]".

3.13 Educate and empower the next generation of workers and managers

The same high-level HSE strategy document[135] recommended that **there is a need to effectively educate and empower the next generation of workers**. The LOcHER project[136] was created, in association with HSE, to support this strategy, and can be used widely in the British industry.

3.14 Management hesitancy

At times, management may be reluctant to invest in adequate levels of OSH. Based on anecdotal evidence, decision makers like buyers, accountants, production managers, and supervisors can exert significant amounts of pressure and influence on the determination of exposure control strategies. Their influence may be directed via elements such as the type of training provided, the extent of investment in OSH, and the types of equipment, PPE and hand-care products selected and bought. Two example situations are described in section 3.10. A visual example in Figure 17 below illustrates a manager's reaction to an OSH decision. It was produced and presented by an operations manager when an occupational hygienist refused to sanction breathing zone (BZ) air sampling before the principles of good practice were implemented[137]. The manager's thoughts were if the operatives were found to be exposed below relevant WELs for the sampled substances, nothing more needed to be done. It is not true, and a concise explanation is in section 1.7.

Figure 17[137] A present to an occupational hygienist who refused to sanction BZ air sampling before adequate exposure control measures were in place.

3.15 Trainers and trainees' preferences

Training approaches failing to adapt to user preferences are not satisfactory for achieving effective communication and RM. Young learners prefer interactive and innovative ways of learning[138,139]. When written information was used, it was more effective when text is limited, and pictures were used[138,139]. Experienced workers will also appreciate the same approach rather than facing wordy presentations, leaflets and slides[140]. Presenting information in multiple formats results in the most 'learning gains'[138,139,140]. An introduction to effective risk communication is presented in chapter 11.

3.16 Inadequate exposure control designs

Employers, some with help from OSH practitioners and specialists, often used inadequate control designs. This is a major issue in COSHH-RM. Experience over the years shows that the quality and adequacy of exposure control measures can be greatly influenced by human and system factors. Examples include:

- Lack of understanding about a pollutant's characteristics, such as particle sizes of dust and their behaviours in air, including the potential for generating explosive atmospheres, being susceptible to electrostatic charges and cross draughts.
- Wrong assumptions about the ways in which pollutants move in the air and onto the skin. For example, a solvent vapour is denser than air, so it will sink to the floor level; dust is not seen in the air close to an activity, so the control at the source must be adequate.

- Failure to appreciate or understand the way LEV hoods and the associated elements work, such as face-velocity, capture (extraction) velocity, capture zone or capture bubble and hood design requirements.

- One-size hood, fitted to an extending and flexible ducting, is used widely as one-size fit all.

- Failure to appreciate or understand the performance limitations and use requirements of different types of Personal Protective Equipment (PPE).

- Limitations linked to 'fitness-to-practice (competency) and attitudes of those devising, designing and/or recommending control measures.

- Potential pressure to reduce short-term costs and get something in place.

- Complicated product standards and guidance documents are difficult to interpret and use by those at the coalface.

On these issues and to support your OSHKE, several visual examples are presented in this book.

3.17 PPE as the first line of exposure control

Often, **PPE on its own may be used without adequate justification or incorrectly selected, used and/or maintained.** Examples of incorrect uses of PPE are presented in Chapters 6 and 7. You will want to carefully observe these examples, reflect on the likely exposure consequences, and, where necessary, take appropriate actions in your area of responsibility.

3.18 Summary

This Chapter sets out some of the challenges and failures that have impinged and have the potential to impinge on adequate exposure control to SHH. Throughout this book, several visual and case study examples are provided to support your efforts in change management.

Chapter 4: An Introduction to Training on Risk Awareness and Undertaking Risk Assessments

"Risk comes from not knowing what you are doing."

- *Warren Buffet, Business Magnate, Investor and Philanthropist.*

4.1 Introduction

We learnt in Chapters 2 and 3 that stimulating[93] and user-centred[138,139,140] awareness training on risk, RA and RM measures is vital for cultivating safe working practices. We know from the Löftstedt[44] review that COSHH-related costly administrative elements included RA, training and record keeping. We also know that a vast majority of GB employers and others asked for simplification of RA/RM procedures, training and record keeping[93, 101-103,109]. When the training is applied boringly, disproportionally or incorrectly, it could cause problems for effective and efficient COSHH-RM and worker health protection. So, at every opportunity, OSH practitioners should strive hard to find ways to improve RA, RM and training effectiveness; reduce costs; help portability of training between employers, and deliver better RoI overall. With a view to providing a supporting hand, this Chapter describes several not-for-profit resources, with commentaries on their strengths and weaknesses.

Training - (i) Essential steps for safe working with substances hazardous to health; (ii) A simple dashboard introducing OSH-RM concepts; (iii) Health Risks at Work. Do you know yours?; and (iv) Learning Occupational Health by Experiencing Risks (LOcHER).

Risk Assessment/Risk Management - (i) An introduction to understanding risk; (ii) An introduction to risk ranking; (iii) COSHH Essentials direct advice sheets; (iv) COSHH Essentials Control Banding approach; (v) COSHH Essential control banding e-tool; and (vi) HSE's RA template.

4.2 Essential steps for safe working with substances hazardous to health

To start with, the key compliance requirements of the COSHH regulations are summarised on six staircase steps using an A3 poster (Figure 18[141]). This first-of-its-kind, visually appealing poster is helpful for communicating, explaining and displaying the COSHH requirements documented in over 100 pages of the COSHH ACoP. To support you further, this poster is integrated within the free-to-use interactive LOcHER presentation on the 'Basics of COSHH'[142]. In addition, the LOcHER website has seven more COSHH-RM related interactive presentations[143]. They could be used in tutor-led training as well as in self-directed learning because they:

- Are interactive,
- Contain notes which are easy to read and understand,
- Use a significant amount of visual content to improve communication effectiveness,
- Incorporate video demonstrations by respected peers,
- Have in-built facilities for checking learning effectiveness, and
- Are useful for cutting training-related costs.

This integrated approach supports the requests for simplification of COSHH training and cost reduction.

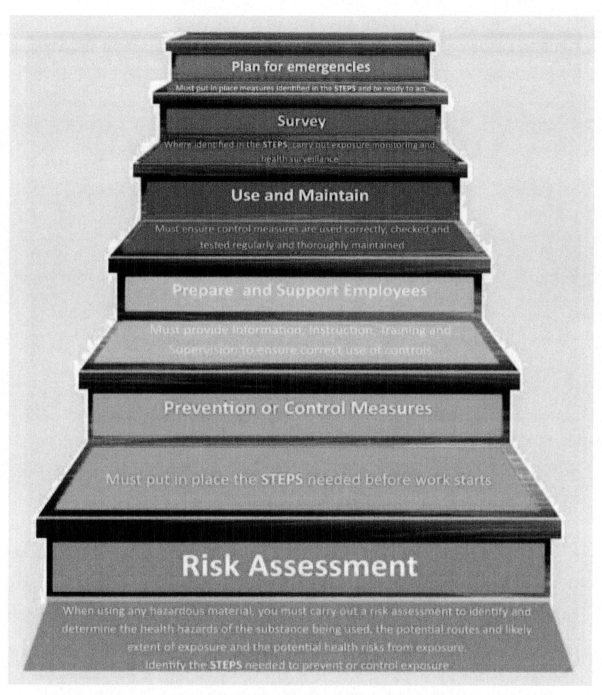

Figure 18[141] Essential steps for safe working with substances hazardous to health.

4.3 A simple dashboard introducing OSH-RM concepts

In Figure 19, a car dashboard[144] lookalike approach is presented for use in training and communication.

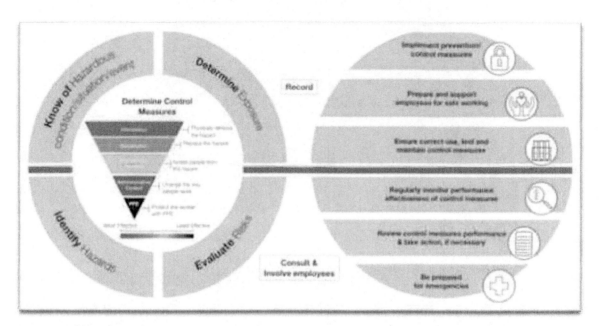

Figure 19[144] A RM dashboard console showing the main steps involved in OSH-RA/RM.

In this Figure:

- RA steps are shown in the lefthand side display monitor of the dashboard, and the control implementation steps are shown in the righthand side monitor,
- Interdependent activities (consultation and record keeping) are shown in the middle of the dashboard console, and
- The interdependency of the two monitors is illustrated using a red bar and intended to project that a quality RA on its own will not deliver adequate control unless RM measures are effective.

Overall, it is a simplified, visually appealing poster. However, it is worth noting that the hierarchy triangle should be presented in the context of the explanation provided in Chapter 1.

4.4 Health Risks at Work. Do you know yours?

This is a multi-award winning free-to-use training resource[145] developed by the Scottish Healthy Working Lives in association with HSE and supported by RoSPA, Scottish Chamber of Safety, SGUK, UK OSH professional bodies, Scottish Trade Union Congress, and many others. The objective of the publication is to support businesses (you) to manage common health risks and to protect their future'. It covers risks to:

- Breathing,
- Skin,
- Muscles, bones and joints,
- Hearing and touch (vibration),
- Wellbeing.

This innovative package has employee friendly short videos and concise Rapid Reference Cards (RRCs) to explain key aspects of RM.

- What should I know?
- What should I do?
- What should I avoid?
- Where can I get help?

It not only provides you with practical information to help you manage health risks by supporting your operations colleagues; it also signposts you to further supporting materials and organisations to give you ongoing support.

4.5 Learning Occupational Health by Experiencing Risks (LOcHER)

The LOcHER[136] has ready-to-use practical and interactive training materials and demonstrations. These were developed by experts in OSH, as well as by young learners in further education colleges and schools. LOcHER materials can be used effectively as a common platform for COSHH training, a way to improve the portability of COSHH training among employers, and for dealing hands-on with Löftstedt's cost related findings.

LOcHER is aimed at supporting your aspirations for developing independent, autonomous learners and employees through active engagement with OSH learning. It is miles better than the 'chalk and board' method. In addition, learners/trainees/employees/employers can showcase[136] their ideas on risk control practices through the LOcHER website; enter and hopefully win competitions organised by SGUK.

The training resources described in Sections 4.2 to 4.5 provide opportunities for 'mix and match'; for meeting the challenges of cost, reducing boredom, improving training effectiveness and accelerating the potential for training portability. The success of the latter is highly dependent on the extent of cooperation between professional bodies and training organisations.

4.6 An introduction to understanding risk

Following the introduction to four user friendly training/communication approaches in the previous sections, this section introduces a widely used concept for understanding/teaching/appreciating risk. Before reading the content of this section, it would be helpful to watch a US-based introductory short video[146]. The statistics quoted are US relevant, which shouldn't distract from the risk relevant explanation.

A hazard may be an object, a hazardous agent, a situation, condition, action or behaviour which has the potential to cause injury and/or ill health to people and/or damage to investment, property and the environment. For example, a block of teak wood is a 'harmless' object. When it is subjected to fine sanding, it can create hardwood dust in the respirable range (less than 10 μm diameter particles), which is a SHH, a respiratory sensitiser and a carcinogen. In another example, a painter, spraying (action) an isocyanate based two-pack paint in a spray booth, lifts the air-fed visor before the booth's spray clearance time has passed. This behaviour can create a situation for exposure to respiratory sensitising isocyanate particles. Similarly, an incorrect/incompetent OSH decision, behaviour or action by operations and OSH practitioners can land an organisation in a Court of law, put employees OSH at peril and put the organisation's investment/cash flow at serious risk.

Risk is part of everything we do. In the context of OSH, it may be explored as uncertainty, whether positive or negative, that will affect the outcome of a person's safety/health, activity or intervention. Described in another way, the risk is the chance that an activity, action or exposure etc., could take place and could cause harm. For example, Toluene diisocyanate is a toxic SHH. If it is kept in a correctly sealed container and stored correctly, the potential for exposure is negligible, and the risk of suffering respiratory sensitisation is negligible. When an isocyanate-based paint is sprayed without suitable RPE being worn, the activity/situation/action can lead to exposure; this, in turn, can present a significant degree of risk of respiratory sensitisation, which can lead to work-related asthma (outcome).

Excessive exposure to a SHH may be expressed as being exposed above 'tolerable' levels, such as WELs[25], COSHH Essentials Control Banding exposure ranges[94], or where required by law[22], the level of exposure is not reduced so far as is reasonably practicable. We now know and accept that the dust trigger values in COSHH regulations are no longer tolerable (Section 1.4). A tolerable level for a SHH is set based on currently available toxicology, pharmacokinetics, practicalities of control, and cost benefit considerations, so caution should be in your mind.

On the other hand, the extent of exposure to a SHH will be influenced and determined by exposure modifying factors, including: (i) physical and chemical properties (for example, solid, liquid, gas, density, the shape of dust/fibres, dustiness, surface tension, viscosity, boiling point); (ii) concentration in air and on the skin or during ingestion; (iii) exposure time and frequency; (iv) site of action. (local or systemic); (v) individual susceptibilities (vi) the effectiveness of and the type of exposure control measures in place; (vi) pharmacokinetics etc.

So, when carrying out COSHH risk assessments, it is necessary to consider these interrelated factors. To make it easy, you may use preprepared advice provided in reliable resources such as HSE's COSHH Essentials direct advice sheets[92] and the COSHH Essentials control banding tool[94]. Alternatively, engage a CP like an occupational hygienist.

Standard of general conditions[50] of a workplace: based on your walkthrough observations, it could be categorised as:

• **Poor**: There appears to be a general failure of compliance across a range of OSH issues, including those matters related to COSHH. For example, failure to address risks arising from issues such as SHH, machinery, transport, manual handling, slips and trips, vibration, noise, consultation, well-being etc. and inadequate welfare facilities. The observations suggest that the employer appears to be deliberately avoiding minimum legal requirements for commercial gain, including failure to seek competent help.

- **Reasonable**: The range of OSH issues appears to be adequately addressed, with only minor omissions/lapses that could lead to exposure. For example, competently designed, installed LEV, and used correctly, but fourteen monthly maintenance and inspections were delayed by two months due to admin related issues; Tight fitting RPE wearers were not facepiece fit tested. No reason to believe that these failures to comply are commercially motivated and is causing immediate concerns for adequate exposure control. The employer involved has now understood the omissions/lapses and indicated immediate actions based on the significance of the risk.

- **Good in general**: Compliance against a range of leading indicators of control effectiveness.

You may categorise **Exposure likelihood** to a SHH using a semi-quantitative approach. One below was designed using the information in HSE's Enforcement Management Model (version 3.2)[50].

- **Unlikely (UL),** Score: 1. Because of the quality of control measures and safe systems of work in place, including controls, training, supervision regime and the *OSH related standard of general conditions* is judged to be '<u>Good in general</u>' (see above), exposure to the hazard is almost unlikely. At all times, all aspects of exposure control measures, including their use, testing and maintenance, meet the recommendations of the applicable HSE guidance for the hazardous condition, event or activity.

- **Likely (L),** Score: 2. Because control measures and safe systems of work are not tight enough to stop the likelihood of exposure taking place, e.g. suitable tight fitting, fit tested respirator is provided but worn by operatives with hair in the face seal region. OSH related standard of general conditions is Judged to be 'reasonable'.

- **Most likely (ML),** Score: 3. The work activity/event/condition/situation can cause exposure because control measures are not present or inappropriate. OSH related standard of general conditions is Judged to be 'poor'. For example, a full-face respirator is worn correctly to enter a 'cleaned/examined' empty degreasing tank, previously contained dichloromethane. What is the problem here? – respirators are unsuitable for entering a confined space because of the foreseeable potential for oxygen deficiency leading to unconsciousness/death, and breathing extensively high concentrations of dichloromethane vapour can cause asphyxiation/death.

Severity of Harm caused (consequence) by work-related exposure to SHH may be placed in three categories[50]:

- **Serious health effect (VSH),** Score: 3. It is credible that a health effect could occur and that can:
o cause permanent, progressive or irreversible conditions.
o cause permanent disabling conditions, leading to a lifelong restriction of work capability or a major reduction in quality of life.
- **Significant health effect (SH),** Score: 2. It is credible that a health effect could occur and could:
o cause non-permanent or reversible health effects;
o causes non-progressive conditions, or
o results in temporary disability.
- **Minor health effect (MH),** Score: 1. It is credible that a health effect could occur and that the injuries or ill health:
o conditions are minor and not included in the two categories above.

Examples of conditions, due to exposure to SHH, that can cause **serious health effects (VSH)**[84] are:

Angiosarcoma of the liver	Skin cancer	Mesothelioma
Cancer of a bronchus or lung	Peripheral neuropathy	Cancer of the urinary tract or the bladder
Skin sensitisation, allergic contact dermatitis; severe skin burns	Chrome ulceration of the nose or throat	Primary carcinoma of the lung where there is accompanying evidence of silicosis
Occupational asthma;	Cancer of the nasal cavity or associated air sinuses	Extrinsic alveolitis (including farmer's lung) Repeated attacks of alveolitis may lead to disabling scarring of the lungs.
Pneumoconiosis	Byssinosis	Asbestosis

Examples of conditions, due to exposure to SHH, that can cause **significant health effects (SH)**[84] are:

Acne	Chrome ulceration of the skin of the hands or forearm
Folliculitis	Irritant contact dermatitis

Examples of conditions due to exposure to SHH that can cause **minor health effects (MH)**[84] are:

- Temporary symptoms like minor irritation of the respiratory system, nausea, headache, and minor skin irritations.

The information provided should help you to introduce pertinent issues involved in a risk assessment and for undertaking RAs. It should help transparency and guidance-based judgements for determining the likelihood of exposure and the potential for the severity of harm to help your RA activities.

Risk assessment (RA) may be expressed as the process of estimating:

- The likelihood *(possibility/probability)* of the occurrence of a specific undesirable event(s). For example, hazardous crystalline silica dust being released into the BZs of workers and the resulting inhalation exposure to that dust; and
- The severity of the harm (e.g. lung cancer) or damage (e.g. loss of permanent quality of life, cost of treating the patient etc.) caused by the exposure to the hazard.

RA involves a value judgement concerning the significance of the outcome. For example, daily exposure to a carcinogenic dust is above tolerable levels, and it happens for almost 5 hours of each working day, no action is taken to control the exposure, so the likelihood of lung cancer is high, and there is a failure to comply with the law.

For practical purposes, COSHH RA/RM may be viewed as consisting of six distinct elements: hazard identification, exposure/risk evaluation; determination of the appropriate control measures based on exposure/seriousness of health risk; implementing/maintaining the control measures;

checking for control effectiveness; and rectifying any shortfalls. This type of dissection should help you examine your RAs in a stepwise fashion.

4.7 An introduction to risk ranking

Based on the information in Section 4.6, a risk ranking model is described in Table 3. It is a simple semi-quantitative linear grading model for raising risk awareness and introducing RA/RM concepts. As the model isn't highly analytical to take account of the subtle variations/complexities influencing exposure likelihood, the model cannot be expected to deliver a highly accurate and precise risk ranking.

Table 3 A semi-quantitative scoring model for raising risk awareness

Exposure likelihood	X	Severity (seriousness) of harm	=	Risk (a semi-quantitative grading)
1 Unlikely (UL)		1 Minor health effect (MH)		1 Minimal 2-3 Low
2 Likely (L)		2 Significant health effects (SH)		4 Medium 6-9 High
3 Most Likely (ML)		3 Serious health effects (VSH)		

To support your OSHKE and to explore the application of the risk ranking model in Table 3, a construction industry kerbstone cutting case study is presented in Table 4. After studying this example, you may use a selection of your workplace activities to become familiar with the model and for use in training sessions.

During kerbstone cutting, stone dressers and others in the work area could become exposed to crystalline silica dust. The effect of exposure to respirable silica dust can result in **serious health effects (VSH).** The exposure can cause multiple diseases, including silicosis, that lead to disability and death. It also causes lung cancer, chronic obstructive pulmonary disease (COPD), and kidney disease. However, by reducing the extent of exposure, the risk of getting the diseases could be minimised. The case study summarised in Table 4 shows that to reduce the risk, suitable and adequate control measures should always remain effective.

Table 4 Kerbstone cutting and risk ranking

Work situation /controls in place	Expected controls	Exposure likelihood	Severity of harm	Risk ranking
Dry cutting. Dust clouds around workers disperse quickly. Fine dust contaminated clothing, tools and work areas.	HSE CIS 54[147] and CN6[148]: Wet cutting or tool extraction and respirator.	3 – Most Likely	3 - VSH	9 - High
Wet cutting. No visible dust clouds. Clothing appears clean. No fine visible layers of dust in work areas.		2 - Likely	3 - VSH	6 - High
Wet cutting. No visible dust clouds. Clothing appears clean. Use high efficiency (FFP3) respirator, not fit tested. Dried up fine layers of dust in the work area.		2 - Likely	3 - VSH	6 - High
Wet cutting. No visible dust around workers. Clothing appears clean. FFP3 respirator, fit tested, cleanshaven operatives. Trained to use tools and equipment. Workers are aware of health hazards and the exposure risks associated with crystalline silica. Effective supervision to ensure the correct use of tools and equipment. Tools and equipment are regularly tested and maintained. Wet slurry to a sump and cutting areas cleared of wet slurry.		1 - UL It cannot always be guaranteed.	3 - VSH	3 - Low

4.8 A case study introduction to risk assessment

Figure 20 An empty bottle of household bleach with its user instruction label and the safety cap system.

As an introduction to RA, household bleach is used for exploring common sense, brevity and simplicity-centred RA. The **hazardous nature** of the product and the SHH in the bleach could be identified using the pictorial hazard warning signs and the written words on the bottle label (Figure 20). Based on the hazard warning signs, the product is corrosive. The written information on the label informs that the corrosivity is due to sodium hypochlorite and sodium hydroxide (main ingredients).

Now, let us consider the **'control measures'** recommended for safely using bleach. It includes protective gloves and face and eye protection. Let us explore the gloves options first. To do this, reflect on household dishwashing gloves and fuel filling gloves available at diesel delivery pumps. Which one would be considered suitable and why?

Washing-up gloves:

(i)   Are recommended for washing/cleaning operations involving household chemicals.

(ii)   Do not have welded seams, whereas the forecourt ones have weakly welded seams, liable to break easily during use, including donning and doffing.

(iii)   It can be selected by size to fit wearers. The other type is a one-size fit-all, designed with highly loose-fitting cuffs and fingers. During use, the one-size fit-all design can cause problems with dexterity and inward leaks (via the short and highly open-design cuffs). Furthermore, inward leakage (penetration) through the weakly welded seems to be a significant possibility.

(iv)   Have a patterned palm to improve grip. The other one doesn't.

(v)   Made from rubber, it can be used with household bleach; the other type is not suitable or adequate for a number of reasons, such as those described above.

Other control measures include: the bent neck with a pointed nose and a narrow hole opening of the nose; the active ingredients are encapsulated in a gel form to help exposure control and for a controlled release of the active ingredients. Furthermore, a safe working distance (SWD) can be maintained by holding the bottle by its body and not close to the bent neck. These measures can help targeted pouring, including around awkward areas in a toilet-pan.

Similarly, the *'prevention'* step could be explained using the safety cap system. It is designed to prevent young children from accessing bleach. It means every time the bottle is closed, the safety system must be applied correctly (a proportionate RM measure), and the correct application will be indicated by a click sound (a nudge). The system, when applied correctly, will also prevent leakage in case the bottle is knocked over.

Another proportionality measure could be explained using one of the recommendations on the label – wear eye/face protection. Many users in homes may not use safety eye/face protection. In doing so, they are not following the user's instruction. At homes, however, bleach is used infrequently and in tiny quantities at a time. The corrosive chemicals (sodium hydroxide and sodium hypochlorite) are encapsulated in a quality gel to prevent/minimise aerosol generation when pouring. The pouring mechanism is designed to control the rate and direction of pouring, which should minimise the potential for exposure. Because of these combined precautions, the potential for eyes becoming exposed (exposure likelihood) to the bleach is unlikely. Okay, there is a potential for aerosol generation during the brush cleaning task. It can be managed by keeping a SWD by choosing a brush with a designed-in aerosol deflector welded to the handle (the lid that covers the brush storage container) and using gentle brushing techniques. However, the manufacturer of the product is following a cover-all scenarios approach for the provision of safety information and, in some ways undertaking 'risk transferring and sharing' (Section 4.2) through user instructions. It includes Dos and Don'ts and 'in case of emergency' instructions. So, a small area of the product label has been used innovatively for conveying the information for RA/RM.

In general, for a vast number of SHH, suitably designed product labels should be able to summarise and communicate information/instructions for RA/RM. For the widely encountered process generated substances, the home is COSHH-Essentials direct advice sheets[92].

4.9 Other risk assessment tools

HSE has published several easy-to-use approaches for simplifying COSHH RA/RM process to promote simple and sensible RM. Examples are described below.

4.10 COSHH Essentials direct advice sheets

Nearly 250 task based direct advice sheets are available (Table 5), covering nineteen industrial sectors[92.] In the absence of a direct advice sheet for your needs, you may use the COSHH Essentials Control Banding tool (Section 4.13).

Recently, HSE has been rationalising and updating existing direct advice sheets to optimise help and support to meet stakeholder requirements established through their research reports[64,65,93,101-103,109,110]. For example, welding sheets were reduced from 21 to 10. The approach is welcome and a positive way forward for improving specificity, clarity of communication, and usability, as well as reducing paper mountain, record keeping and the time required to become familiar with direct advice sheets.

Table 5 Industry sectors and COSHH Essentials exposure control direct advice sheets[92].

Industry sectors and Direct advice sheets				
(Numbers in brackets show how many sheets were available on 20 December, 2021)				
Agriculture (Farming) (10)	Flour (Bakers and millers) (8)	Metalworking fluids (5)	Microelectronics (6)	Motor Vehicle Repair (5)
Printing (50)	Rubber (7)	Offshore (36)	Service and Retail (29)	Woodworking (18)
Welding (10)	Dichloromethane (DCM) (4)			
Silica dust and related industry sectors				
Brick and tile (7)	Ceramics (6)	Construction (10)	Stonework (8)	Quarries (9)
Foundry (15)	Manufacturing (4)			

Recently updated sheets, e.g. Welding Fume WL3 sheet[149], provide information under the following lead subtitles, making it easy for you.

- What this sheet covers
- Hazards. This section includes the harm that can be caused
- (Exposure control) equipment and procedures
- LEV
- RPE
- Skin exposure control (not a separate subheading)
- General ventilation
- Commissioning, maintenance, examination and testing of LEV
- Health surveillance
- Training and supervision
- Employee checklist

4.11 When using COSHH Essentials direct advice sheets

Although the direct advice sheets recommend exposure control measures, users need to consider what is happening in their workplaces and compare them with the recommended control measures. It is important to make sure that:

- Control measures recommended in a chosen sheet can be applied to your industrial sector.

- Controls to be used are appropriate for the task/work procedures and practices at your workplace.

- You can follow all the points described in the sheet.

- You can implement the controls in a sheet easily and without further competent help from other professionals like occupational hygienists and LEV designers.

- You have access to a competent LEV installer.

If the answer to any of the above is 'no' or 'not sure', use other effective measures, such as seeking help from a relevant trade body or suitable CP. Correctly implementing and maintaining the recommended controls means an employer will normally be doing enough to comply with COSHH regulations. Figure 12 in this book provides a helpful route map for making this assessment.

When designing and implementing the recommended engineering controls (normally illustrated as line diagrams in direct advice sheets), take into account the following:

- When different types of engineering control measures are recommended, as in WL3[149], you or another responsible person should identify the appropriate option(s) for your situation. When selecting the option(s), you should consult operatives and supervisors who will be directly involved in the task and will be using the control measures.
- A diagrammatic illustration of a control measure is intended to help in designing, constructing, installing, and testing the control measure. During the design phase, CPs should (i) consult operatives and managers who will use the control measure; (ii) consider relevant local issues such as the way work is carried out, the environment in which the work will be undertaken, conditions such as flammability, electrostatic charges, cross draughts, etc.
- Based on relevant information, a CP should create 'draughtsman design drawings', which should be used for the construction, installation and performance testing after installation.
- If the selected engineering control is bought as an off-the-shelf product, CPs or a responsible person must ensure that it is fit for purpose.
- One-size hoods that fit all situations and are attached to an extending arm extraction duct (sometimes known as an elephant trunk) are highly limited in their application and performance (Figures 23 and 24). Therefore, you, CP or the responsible person should pay close attention when choosing this type of capture hood.
- Trained and supervised operatives should use control measures correctly.
- Control measures should be regularly tested and maintained by CPs.
- Leading indicators may be used for assessing control effectiveness.

A similar quality assurance system should be in place for RPE and other types of PPE. To illustrate the importance of competent decision making, three statements from WL3[149] are reproduced below for your reflection and application.

- Select an appropriate design of hood to maximise the fume capture from your welding process by considering its shape, size or hood diameter and whether flanged capture hoods can be used.
- RPE may be needed where fume extraction alone cannot provide adequate control and when welding outdoors.
- RPE may also be needed in situations when the LEV system is not able to achieve and maintain consistent capture of the fume generated.

These three statements clearly convey HSE instruction that a CP/responsible person should decide:

- when and how to use LEV/RPE and
- LEV or RPE selected is adequate and suitable for the job, the user/wearer and the environment in which it is to be used.

It is important to note that incorrect selection and use can lead to injuries, ill health and, in the worst case, death. So, OSH practitioners involved in recommending exposure control measures and checking their effectiveness carry a big responsibility, even when employer liability insurance or professional indemnity insurance is in place.

OSHKE

1.   Do you always check, assess and ensure that each of the control measures chosen and put in place is adequate and suitable for the: task/job, work activity/process, users and work environment?

2.   Do you take account of the above points in your RAs and calibrate them for proportionality, prudence, usability and, where required by law, to reduce exposure as low as is reasonably practical?

4.12 Examples of potential consequences of incorrect decisions made when designing, installing and using control measures

It would be wrong to assume that every OSH practitioner or SME employer can design, install and implement every type of control measure recommended in COSHH Essentials direct advice sheets and in other types of HSE guidance. Where necessary, engaging the right CPs is vitally important and a legal requirement. Failing to follow important points, such as those described in the previous section, can lead to exposure control failures. They, in turn, can create the potential for operatives to be 'excessively exposed' to SHH, which can lead to health risks, non-compliance with the law, wasted resources and the need to invest more financial and time resources to rectify shortcomings. Seven visual examples are shown below, and several related issues are discussed. Examine these in detail and reflect so that mistakes of this kind can be avoided during your watch.

Figure 21[150] A poor LEV 'receiving hood' design.

Figure 21 shows that the hood is fixed to a wall at a specific height (take note of the square and triangular-shaped fixing brackets). Suction within this small hood is created at three places!!! The extent of dust capture is poor, which causes a significant amount of dust to escape sideways and away from the hood. The task area may be suffering from an intense side draught. Fine dust can be seen on surfaces, including on the outside surface of the LEV hood and its ducting. There are wheel and foot marks on the floor, created due to the presence of a thin layer of fine dust. The design and installation arrangements do not give confidence that the hood was competently designed and installed to deliver compliance and value for money. There is a failure to comply with the principles of good practice. Whoever was involved in this project has questions to answer on exposure control failures, wasted resources and poor RoI.

OSHKE

LEV hood design with reference to Figure 21.

(i) As the bin is a roll-in, roll-out type, how will you tackle the redesigning of the LEV hood without causing excessive suction of the product into the hood? *Here are some thoughts: The first question would be, am I a CP to design the hood? Get to know the physical and chemical properties of the dust; understand the task, process flow and substance handling methods; speak to operations; calculate capture/receiving distance, determine capture bubble area, airflow requirements and the size and the configuration of the hood; decide how best to mount it to facilitate bin roll-in-roll-out and much more. How to prevent SHH from spreading to other areas during roll-in/roll-out. If the hood is to be designed as a receiving hood, many other factors should be considered. If you are engaging CPs, put these issues to them.*

(ii) If you are one of these: an OHS General Practitioner or an Occupational Hygiene General Practitioner, or an engineering technician (without knowledge and expertise in LEV designing, including creating precision engineering drawings for the manufacture of LEV hoods and LEV systems as a whole), - would you consider yourself as a competent LEV/hood designer? *You decide. My answer is no.*

(iii) Do you think that the designer of the hood shown in Figure 21 would have had a good discussion with operatives before embarking on the design? *Unlikely or ignored the information provided.*

(iv) Looking at the way the hood was installed, do you think that the installer of the hood is a CP? *Unlikely.*

(v) If you consider 'Yes' to (iv) above, what factors would have caused the installer to install the hood in the way seen? *May be a contract job to install the hood, and the installer may not have been trained in LEV design, installation, testing and use.*

(vi) Do you think that there would have been an LEV/hood commissioning report? *Unlikely. This hood needs a 'do not use' sticker right now.*

Figures 22[151] Inappropriate movable hood as control

It is probable that the movable extraction hood, shown in Figure 22, may have been installed as an afterthought. It may be an attempt to rectify the pollutant control problem; to pacify potential industrial relations issues or some other reason. It appears that the captor hood is inadequate (the hood is marked with a red arrow to show its position in relation to the cutting tool of the machine). It is attached to an elephant trunk duct with two sharp bends. What would these bends mean for the transport velocity and dust transportation in the duct? *Inefficient LEV operation.*

Figure 23[152] An inadequate and unsuitable engineering control design. Do you agree? Using recommendations in COSHH Essentials direct advice sheets goes hand-in-hand with competent design, installation and use.

Compare the design shown in Figure 23 with the dust control approach shown in COSHH Essentials direct advice sheets on bag opening, tipping and dough mixing (FL1)[153]. The illustration is reproduced in Figure 24 below.

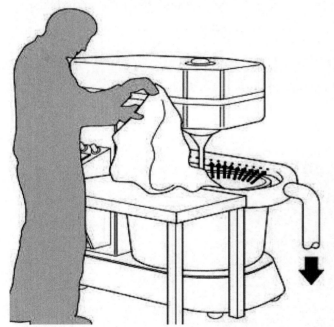

Figure 24[153] A line diagram showing a typical LEV design for bag emptying and powder mixing operation.

The mixing bin can be easily moved away from the ring ventilation design and brought back when needed. The bag can be rested on the bench, and the edge of the bag can be opened, tipped and emptied with the help of the LEV capture zone. Good working practices are vital for the effective use of the extraction system. The empty bag handling system is not shown in this Figure, a weakness.

Figure 25 A cross-cut saw used without LEV hose[154] (watch a demo in the YouTube link) and a dust collection system, such as a portable industrial-grade vacuumcleaner[155].

HSE created this 'setup' video for a demonstration. They have another video showing the difference when the LEV is made to work correctly[156]. After viewing this film, what did you observe in terms of dust control efficacy when using LEV? - watch the very end of the film carefully.

OSHKE

With reference to the two YouTube films you watched, if the cutting task lasts 20 seconds and is done 10 -12 times over the day, would you demand that the operator wears a power assisted reusable respirator with helmet mounted hood? *Surely the decision should be risk based and not hazard based (wood dust is an asthmagen). Does the hazard-based RM ring familiar?*

Figure 26[157] Cutting stone with a powered rotary saw (the authors, of reference 157 quoted the source as HSE). The situation shows failures to apply good control practices to minimise emission, spread and exposure, slips, trips and falls and lots more.

OSHKE

With reference to Figure 26.

1.   Print Table 7 in LEV guidance ([HSG258](HSG258))[127], with its help, list the obvious design shortcomings with the receiving hood LEV shown in Figure 26.

2.   Should the design be a partially enclosing hood? *Yes. It should enclose the workpiece as much as possible, which is not the case with the design shown in Figure 26. Three "bonnets" like hoods are seen; are they partial enclosures?*

3.   Would you point the finger at the worker for not using the hood? *No.* The design of the LEV receiving hoods, the work, clothing storage, lighting etc., provides evidence for the poor design of the work area/process and RM measures.

4.   Compare this hood design with the one recommended in the COSHH Essentials direct advice sheet ST3[158], reproduced in Figure 27 below. What design features stand out in Figure 27? *Partial enclosure, turntable, and a workbench. It is hoped that the turntable provided would be height adjustable to accommodate varying sizes of workpieces. The enclosure hood face width should accommodate workpieces/work practices requirements. The depth of the hood should be adequate to improve air extraction efficiency and reduce eddies at the opening (face) of the enclosure. On the line diagram, there is an angled extraction slotted port is shown - to receive fast-moving dust clouds away from the hood. Duct extraction velocity should be fast enough to suck the dust cloud as soon as it is fed to the hood.*

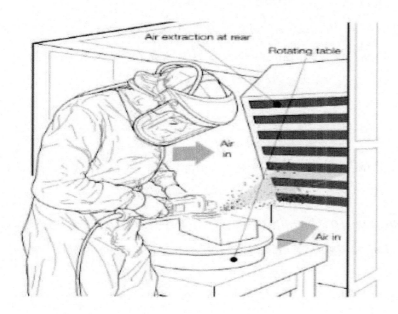

Figure 27[158] A partially enclosing hood design with work station and a turntable

Figure 28[157] COSHH Essential direct advice sheet (WL3[149]) recommended control option used incorrectly (the authors of reference 157 quoted the source as HSE).

Identify the obvious incorrect use as seen in this Figure. How many times have you witnessed LEV hood installation leading to 'head in contaminated air', as in this Figure. Why is the fume not seen?

Figure 29 shows a paint mixing reactor vessel with the port sealer removed. After an automated solvent washing process, under controlled conditions (hardware and software), a quality assurance tester (not shown) manually checked the insides of the vessel for any residual paint left behind. The tester, wearing a half mask respirator, looked through the opening (face placed almost within the opening) to examine the insides of the reactor. The activity failed to integrate hardware, software and human factors to comply with COSHH's good

control practices. A similar situation can be seen in reference 159. In many quality assurance situations where solvent vapours were involved, failure to use safe systems of work resulted in fatalities and serious injuries.

OSHKE

With reference to Figure 29, could the 'checking' job be accomplished in other ways? *What about an intrinsically safe lamp with a camera, like those used for testing the internal conditions of pipes and sewers? What about a mirror, like those used by dentists and test engineers, of suitable size and designed for examining the insides of the paint making reactor? Remember intrinsic safety.*

4.13 A description of the principles underpinning the COSHH Control Banding approach for inhalation exposure control

The COSHH Essentials Control Banding (CB) is a generic RA scheme for controlling inhalation exposure to SHH[94]. It was **developed by an HSE-working group** involving experts from the Confederation of British Industry, Trade Union Congress, BOHS and other independent experts[94]. CB approach was developed with the intention of providing practical and reliable advice to SMEs and General Practice OSH practitioners without access to competent occupational hygiene skills. It operates in a 'screening' mode, which means that it is both inherently conservative and identifies situations where access to more specialised approaches from experts is advisable.

This section provides key information on the CB approach, which should make it easy for you to gain an appreciation of the approach. The CB approach is made possible because:

- It is feasible to group manufactured hazardous substances/products into **Health Hazard Groups (HHGs)** based on their health hazard H-Statements (those beginning with 3, such as 301, 315) assigned to them by the manufacturer or supplier[95]. The robustness of this HHG grouping has been evaluated[95,98].

- Expert analysis by the HSE-WG showed that the "**exposure potential**" can be determined based on the amount used and the dustiness or volatility of the substance/product. Several peer reviewed assessments were undertaken to verify the WG findings, these include references 159-164.

- There are only a few fundamentally different **mechanical control approaches (CAs)**, - namely general ventilation, engineering control (LEV) and containment (full/partial enclosures).

- Many of the control problems have been met and solved before[165], enabling appropriate CAs to be determined based on HHGs and exposure potential.

However, it is important to note that actual exposure level - instant, peak or TWA concentrations (for example, 5 mg/m3 or 5 ppm) in the workplace - will depend on several other factors, such as correct design, use, testing and maintenance of control measures, and administrative and behaviour-based decisions. The influence of these various effects is already demonstrated pictorially in Figures 21 to 29.

It is not, therefore, advisable to use the CB approach to determine the actual exposure level on a given day or an hour. It would be wrong and potentially dangerous to believe that employers have only to put the recommended Control Approach (CA) hardware in place to achieve adequate control. So far, we have explored, with the help of several workplace examples, the importance of correct selection, design, installation, use, checks and maintenance of the hardware. Their performance observations form part of exposure control effectiveness determination.

The elements of the CB approach are summarised in Tables 6 to 11 below. A detailed description can be found in reference 94. If you are not familiar with the approach, study the information in this section and practice the application of the approach using a few workplace examples, including the one in section 4.14.

Table 6 The Principles involved in the COSHH Essentials Control Banding (CB).

HEALTH HAZARD		EXPOSURE POTENTIAL		GENERIC RISK ASSESSMENT	CONTROL APPROACH (CA)
Substance or products allocated to a **Health Hazard Group (HHG)**, based on health-related H-statements in Table 7. When a substance with multiple **H-statements** and allocated to different HHGs, the final selection will be determined by the worst case HHG.		Substance allocated to a dustiness or volatility band (Low, Medium or High), **and** amount used band (Small, Medium or Large). Decisions on the above will lead to: **Exposure potential** (Tables 8 and 9).		Using the model in Table 11, combine **HHG** with **exposure potential** factors to determine the degree of control needed. HSE-WG experts' judgements have been applied and peer reviewed papers published.	Hardware approach needed for control (1 of 4, below) 1. General ventilation 2. Engineering control 3. Containment 4. Specialist advice **CA** determination is arrived after a generic assessment using **HHG** and **exposure potential**.

Table 7 Allocating substances to HHGs based on H-Statements.

Health Hazard Groups (HHG) and substances health characteristics	Exposure type	Acceptable concentration range	Units	H-statements allocated
A May cause skin/eye irritation; inhalation harm, causes drowsiness	Dust	>1 to 10	mg/m3	H303, H304, H313, H315, H316, H319, H320, H333, H336 EU66
	Vapour	>50 to 500	ppm	
B Causes harm by inhalation; skin contact, ingestion	Dust	>0.1 to 1	mg/m3	H302, H312, H332, H371, EU71
	Vapour	>5 to 50	ppm	
C Toxic, corrosive, respiratory irritant	Dust	>0.01 to 0.1	mg/m3	H301, H311, H314, H317, H318, H331, H335, H370, H373
	Vapour	>0.5 to 5 ppm	ppm	
D Very toxic, toxic to reproduction	Dust	<0.01	mg/m3	H300, H310, H330, H351, H360, H361, H362, H372
	Vapour	<0.5	ppm	
E Very toxic, toxic to reproduction	Dust	-	mg/m3	H334, H340, H341, H350, EU70
	Vapour	-	ppm	

Table 8: Solids exposure potential- Factors used in the determination of the amount used and the dustiness.

Amount used		Dustiness	
Grammes	Small	Pellet does not break up. Little evidence of any dust was observed during use.	Low
Kilogrammes	Medium	Granular or crystalline solids. When used, dust is seen, but it settles out quickly. Dust on surfaces after use.	Medium
Tonnes	Large	Fine and light powders. When used, dust clouds can be seen to form and remain airborne for several minutes.	High

Table 9 Liquid exposure potential - Factors used in the determination of volatility and the amount used.

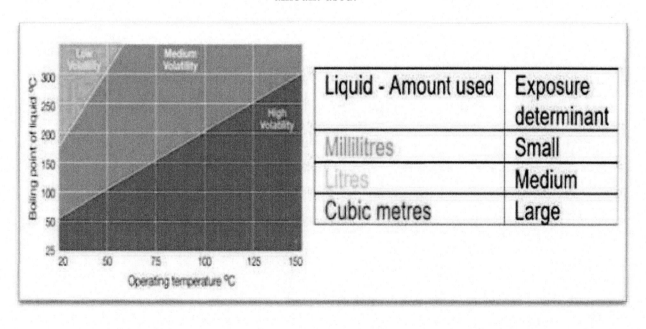

81

Table 10: A description of the control approach and types of hardware.

Control Approach (CA)	Type	Description
1	General ventilation	A "good standard" of ventilation with good working practices. It can be natural ventilation, from doors, windows etc. or controlled, where the air is supplied and/or removed by a powered fan.
2	Engineering control	Typically, LEV. This ranges from a single point extraction close to the dust or vapour to extracted partial enclosures such as booths. It includes other engineering control methods such as vapour cooling coils, refuges and water suppression.
3	Containment	The substance is largely enclosed in an extracted enclosure. Small breaches may be acceptable, for example, for sampling.

Table 11: Control Approaches based on generic assessment.

Amount used	Low volatility or low dustiness	Medium volatility	Medium dustiness	High volatility or High dustiness
Health Hazard Group (HHG) A substances				
Small	1	1	1	1
Medium	1	1	1	2
Large	1	1	2	2
Health Hazard Group (HHG) B substances				
Small	1	1	1	1
Medium	1	2	2	2
Large	1	2	3	3
Health Hazard Group (HHG) C substances				
Small	1	2	1	2
Medium	2	3	3	3
Large	2	4	4	4
Health Hazard Group (HHG) D substances				
Small	2	3	2	3
Medium	3	4	4	4
Large	3	4	4	4
Health Hazard Group (HHG) E substances				
All amounts	4	4	4	4
Note: Numbers in the box give the type of **Control Approach***:* **1** - General ventilation; **2** - Engineering control; **3** - Containment; **4** - Specialist advice				

4.14 A worked example using the paper-based CB

The CB approach is easy to use, providing the principles are understood correctly. In this section, an example is described to explore its applicability. It involves an organic solvent-based surface coating paint. Information needed to use the CB approach was extracted from the paint product safety data sheet, and a summary is presented in the left-hand column of Table 12.

A description of a hypothetical task:

Paint will be sprayed for coating steel, aluminium, wood, and GRP components.

- Items to be sprayed will be moved to the spray area by a conveyor and moved out by the same means to the baking area.
- It is estimated that about 6 to 8 litres of paint will be used each day.
- A competent spray painter will use high-volume low-pressure spray-painting equipment.
- The painter does this work daily for 5 hours each day.
- Installation of a fully automated robotic system was discounted based on production rate and proportionality.
- The paint is made of a mixture of solids (35%) and organic solvents (65%). The product at room temperature is a highly viscous liquid containing solids. Therefore, the description of the solid (Table 8) will not apply. The paint is considered a liquid for practical purposes because it is a pourable material (liquid containing solids).
- As the activity involves spray painting, the significant inhalation exposure potential is from mist-solvent vapours and particulates. Providing that the exposure to solvent vapours is adequately controlled, inhalation exposure to particulate aerosols should also be under control when using suitable and adequate engineering control measures.
- Where RA determines, suitable RPE may be required. RPE determination is not covered by the CB approach described in section 4.13. It is a weakness of the CB model, but a suitable RPE selector based on CB is described in Chapter 5.

Table 12 Information needed for using the CB approach was extracted from a safety data sheet and summarised below.

Purpose: Professional application of a surface coating	Author's comments on the usefulness of the information in the safety data sheet for using the CB approach – inhalation
Hazard Identification	
Product classification: Mixture (solids and liquids)	Relevant information for using the CB
Hazardous ingredients: Hydrocarbons (C9-C11), n-alkanes, isoalkanes, cyclics	Not so relevant because it isn't easy to understand at the coalface
H-Statements: H226 (flammable liquid and vapour) and *H336* (May cause drowsiness or dizziness). Manufacturer provided an additional H statement, H361, see below	Relevant information **H336: CB HHG** for this H-statement is **A,** (Table 7) (H-361 statement is not relevant for Inhalation exposure control)
Composition information: Additional to hazardous ingredients already stated above. 2-ethyl hexanoic acid, zirconium salt. H361 (Suspected of damaging fertility <u>if swallowed</u>. Suspected of damaging to the unborn child <u>if swallowed</u>)	**H361: CB HHG** is **D,** (Table 7). Relevant information for ingestion
Label's pictograms: Flammability and exclamation mark (harmful/irritant)	Relevant information
Boiling point and vapour pressure: Not provided	Missing relevant information
Precautions	
Prevention: Keep away from heat, hot surfaces, sparks, open flames and other ignition sources. No smoking. Wear protective gloves. Wear eye or face protection. Use only outdoors or in a well-ventilated area. Wear an appropriate respirator when ventilation is inadequate.	Not so Relevant information for CB inhalation exposure assessment Not very helpful. Is it?

Engineering: Use only with adequate ventilation. Use process enclosures, local exhaust ventilation, or other engineering controls to keep worker exposure to airborne contaminants below any recommended or statutory limits. The engineering controls also needed to keep gas, vapour or dust concentrations below any lower explosive limits. Use explosion-proof ventilation equipment.	Relevant information, but several control options were provided. They will require competent help to understand

Information in Table 12 (needed for using the CB approach) was extracted from a safety data sheet provided by the paint manufacturer. As can be seen from Table 12, the person who prepared the safety data sheet has taken a decision that H-Statement, H361 is not relevant for inhalation exposure control because the risk associated with H361 comes from ingestion. This decision may be considered as correct. However, we will use two scenarios to explore the application of the CB approach. **In scenario 1**, All the health relevant health hazard H-statements, H336 and H361, are applied.

Most importantly, the safety data sheet, as prepared, is extremely user unfriendly for coalface users, but may satisfy the requirements of the CLP[24] law.

CE application scenario 1:

- Relevant HHGs are A (for H336) and D (for H361) (Table 7); Therefore, the worst-case HHG is D.
- Amount used is 6 to 8 litres. It equates to Medium (Table 8).
- Volatility is high, based on the H-Statement for flammability (H226), and during spraying, fine vapour will be present. This decision was taken by applying the competency envelope of the author as the boiling point was not provided in the safety data sheet.

Inputting the above information into the CB model (Table 11) leads to a **CA** recommendation: Specialist advice (CA 4). It is anticipated that the specialist, such as an occupational hygienist, would discount H361 because it is not relevant for airborne inhalation exposure control. This anticipation would suggest that the specialist would opt for suitable engineering control, such as an open-faced water wash spray booth, with an in/out access for a motorised rail to convey the items being sprayed.

CE application scenario 2:

In this scenario, H361 is discounted as it is not relevant for inhalation exposure. Therefore, the relevant HHGs is A; **Amount used is Medium**; and **Volatility is high**. When applying the above information to the CB model, the CA recommendation is 'Engineering control' (CA 2). A CP should decide what type of engineering control is needed by taking into account of work rate, the way workpieces are handled, and the environment in which it is used. They should also consult those involved in the work and the information in the safety data sheet.

Based on expertise, water washed partially enclosed spray booth would be appropriate to make it easy to access workpieces. The booth design should take into account flammability. The next stage involves the engineering design of the booth by a competent engineering control designer, followed by manufacturing, installation and testing. Alternatively, a suitable prefabricated booth may be purchased in consultation with a CP.

The above example demonstrates that the CB approach can be used as a screening model by SMEs and General Practice OSH practitioners, but the recommended control approach should be designed, installed, tested and maintained by CPs. When a partially enclosing booth control approach is compared with the COSHH-Essentials direct advice sheet G221[166], a similarity emerges.

4.15 COSHH control banding e-tool

An e-tool resides on the HSE website and can be accessed via Getting started – COSHH e-tool (hse.gov.uk)[167]. At present, the tool, which was developed many years ago, is not easy to use with products involving solids and liquids (like the example in the previous section), gases or process generated substances. When a product has more than one SHH, each substance should be assessed individually, which can take time, the manual CB tool, in section 4.13, does not suffer from this problem. It is possible that HSE may update the e-tool to improve versatility and useability.

4.16 HSE's RA template

HSE RA template[168] is shown in Figure 30 below. It is a simple platform to help employers keep effective records of:

- What are the hazards?
- Who might be harmed by exposure to the hazards, and how?
- What is being done to control the risks?
- What further actions will, if any, be needed to control the risks?
- Who needs to carry out the actions?
- When are the actions needed by?

Risk assessment template — Health and Safety Executive

| Company name: | | Assessment carried out by: | |
| Date of next review: | | Date assessment was carried out: | |

What are the hazards?	Who might be harmed and how?	What are you already doing to control the risks?	What further action do you need to take to control the risks?	Who needs to carry out the action?	When is the action needed by?	Done

Figure 30[168] HSE's risk assessment template published in 2019.

This template[168], in Microsoft Word format, can be downloaded from the HSE website and may be used for managing RAs associated with tasks involving exposure to SHH. It should help OSH practitioners and SME employers to:

- Standardise their RA recordings,
- Monitor the progress of RM implementation, and

- Effectively communicate the RM information to employees and sub-contractors.

You may use this template along with CE direct advice sheets to create task-based RA sheets in 'Microsoft-Word' and store them in an organised "File Explorer" folder or similar, helping to reduce RA related costs and improve efficiency and flexibility. To explain and promote the usefulness of the template, HSE has published six worked examples[168]. With this RA template, the regulator is encouraging task-based RAs, and RM approaches for minimising the paper mountain and saving money and time for SME employers. OSH practitioners should take advantage of the HSE backed approach and maximise the use of the template.

For those having second thoughts about adopting the HSE standardised template, be positive and be nudged. Using standardised templates is not new among professionals. For example, medical doctors use the NHS standardised prescription form; police forces use a standardised form for issuing road traffic offences 'tickets'; and solicitors use Law Society standardised forms for house conveyancing.

4.17 Summary

This Chapter explored the usefulness and utility of several user-friendly tools for supporting OSH practitioners. These included an A3 poster for summarising the requirements of COSHH explained in 100 pages of COSHH ACoP, COSHH Direct Advice Sheets on hazards that can cause serious health effects due to exposure, and HSE's task-based risk assessment template. These tested and tried tools were developed in response to research findings and stakeholder requests for simplification of COSHH-related support materials. It is considered that the resources described in this Chapter and in others can provide support in training, RA and RM steps for a vast majority of situations. Where you need/decide to use alternatives, it is prudent to take account of the issues highlighted in this Chapter and in Chapters 2 and 3 and ensure that the alternatives are proportional and commensurate to the risk being managed.

Chapter 5 Local Exhaust Ventilation in COSHH Risk Management

"Experience has shown that serious mistakes are frequently made in the design of fan ventilation."
- *Haldane, Osborn and Ritchie. Authors of the 2nd report on Ventilation of Factories and Workshops, 1907.*

5.1 Introduction

Workplace air contaminated with SHH could be <u>energised</u>, <u>induced</u> (persuaded/directed) **and <u>taken away</u> from the BZ of operators.** If these three elements can be made to work properly and in association with LEV, workers' exposures could be better controlled. HSE's short video[169] explains the basics of LEV. Every OSH practitioner who deals with COSHH-RM should be familiar with its content and be aware of the importance of correct design, installation, use and maintenance of LEV.

In many workplaces, LEV, in particular hoods and general ventilation (mechanical types), fail to deliver satisfactory control for a variety of reasons. Often due to failure to incorporate simple engineering design and installation principles, some of which were explored in the previous Chapter. Incorrect use and maintenance are two other problems. In this Chapter, some more commonly encountered design/use related issues are discussed. OSH practitioners involved in COSHH-RM should become familiar with these types of errors and make sure they do not happen on their watch.

Jobs associated with LEV – designing, installing, maintaining, testing, including the fourteen monthly examinations, testing and certification – are for competent people in each of these areas. This book is not the place for an extensive discussion on these matters. As a starting point, OSH practitioners can consult HSE guidance HSG408[170]. It provides help on buying LEV and getting the best out of LEV consultants. BOHS P601[171] helps towards developing competency on LEV testing and examination. P602[172] is for understanding the basic design principles of LEV systems and the P604[173] is for those undertaking the commissioning of a LEV system.

5.2 Understanding sucking and blowing in ventilation systems

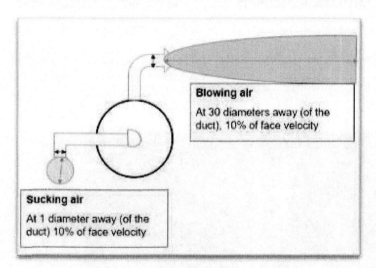

Figure 31 An illustration showing one of the main differences between sucking and blowing.

There is a colossal difference between sucking and blowing air using a ventilation system. You would have experienced this when using a household vacuum cleaner. The differences in magnitude can be demonstrated easily by holding your open hand 15 cm away from your mouth and blowing towards it. On your hand, you will feel the air movement and the force behind it. Still holding your hand at 15 cm, now breath-in as hard as you can. Do you feel the air close to the hands being sucked away? Definitely not! Similarly, you could blow out a candle flame 15 cm away from your mouth, but at the same distance, you will not be able to cause any disturbance to the flame by breathing hard (sucking). Now try with fine tissue paper tinsels or a small amount of thinly spread talcum powder on the surface of a table.

Figure 31 provides an illustrative explanation of the differences between the air being blown and sucked by a ventilation system. In this example, if the face velocity at the duct outlet face is 0.5 m/second and the duct's internal diameter is 5 cm. Air blown out will have about 10% of the face velocity (i.e. 0.05 m/s) at ~30 duct diameter distance (i.e. 150 cm) away from the duct face. If the air is sucked (extracted), 10% of the face velocity will be felt at ~1 duct diameter (i.e. 5cm) away from the duct face – marked with a grey circle in the Figure.

5.3 Contaminant capture zone

In order to extract contaminated air into a LEV hood, the source generating the air contaminant must be within the capture bubble/zone of the hood, as illustrated in Figure 32 below. **A captor**

91

hood capture zone is associated with capture velocity[127]. It is the velocity, outside the face of a capturing hood, necessary to capture the SHH in air, farthest away from the hood face (opening) when the SHH is released from the contaminant generating source. In Figure 32, stone dust is used for a visual presentation. The fine dust was made visible by shining an intense light and using a reduced background lighting around the exhibit in Figure 32.

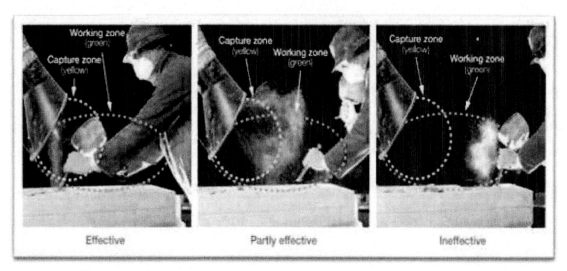

Figure 32[127] Demonstrating capture and working zones when stone dressing work is undertaken.

Capture velocity and the capture bubble are meaningful only with a defined distance between the source and the hood face, as demonstrated in Figure 32 above. More details on capture distance and capture velocity can be found in HSG258[127]. Now, watch HSE demonstration film[174] in which smoke is used to assess the capture bubble of a captor hood. In this demonstration, watch out for a helpful, practical, cost-effective, proportionate, and nonbureaucratic suggestion for marking the capture distance of a hood – *A label marked with capture distance.*

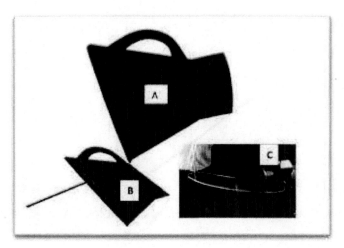

Figure 33 Ideas for indicating a captor hood's capture zone.

In Figure 33, **Item A:** An extraction hood without any facility to exhibit its capture distance. **Item B:** A fold-back type, brown coloured capture distance indicator is attached to a hinge welded onto the extraction hood. **Item C:** A yellow wire capture distance indicator is attached to an extraction hood. As in item B, if necessary the yellow wire indicator could be folded back during work. These types of indicators can act as positive nudges in training demonstrations and at work to encourage users to work within the capture zone, so long as the employer/CP has designed the hood to be suitable and adequate for use with workpieces, the way work is done (Figure 32), and the capture velocity generated is sufficient to extract the contaminant released within the capture zone. Another thing to note is the eddy (edge or whirling) effects of air at the face of a hood. Flanges are helpful to minimise the effect, see Figure 33 and watch How LEV capture hoods work.

OSHKE - Capture distance indicator:

1.   Can you think of ways to displaying capture distance and capture bubble? *What about a laser pointer with adjustable focal length; a flashing LED light with adjustable and lockable focal length so that they could be attached to a captor hood (an idea that likens to a bicyclist light)? Any lighting system should be compatible with intrinsic and other safety issues of the working environment. As a guide, a capture hood is effective when the contaminant cloud is within two hood-diameter from its face.*

2.   Do you mark your LEV hoods with their respective capture/receiving distance? If not, explore the reasons and take action to rectify shortfalls. Also, see HSG 258[127] for recommended face velocities.

5.4 A poor understanding of capture zone

Figure 34[130] An unsuitable LEV design for solvent dispensing and vapour exposure control. The capture bubble of the hood isn't anywhere close to the solvent dispensing point. It is tucked away elsewhere.

Figure 34 shows a lid partially covering the mixing bucket opening. It would help reduce vapour emission into the BZ of the worker, but not enough. The movable extraction hood that should have been placed close to the lid is tucked away and not moved close to the lid (observe the hood attached to a bent flexible ducting and facing away from the operator). This LEV hood was designed for dual use - for the filling operation and the mixing operation – the mixing paddle can be seen just in front of the operator and below the tucked away hood. The hood is a user-unfriendly design. Do you agree? In any case, the capture distance/bubble of the hood is well away from the solvent dispensing point, making it useless. This ineffective system is good for wasting heat, electricity and money. Another control issue: a broom may be used for sweeping up fine dust on the floor. There are many other visible OSH shortcomings. Note the general standard of cleanness and storing practices in the area. They are good visual indicators of poor control/RM.

OSHKE

1.   After a curiosity-based walkthrough observation of the area seen in Figure 34, would you consider BZ personal air monitoring to conclude that the LEV system design is not appropriate or inadequate and the employer has failed to implement COSHH 'good control practice'? *A 360-degree curiosity walk through survey would conclude that there is a need for a root and branch reappraisal of RM measures.*

5.5 Fast moving contaminant clouds and inefficient control

Fast-moving and work activity energised contaminant clouds, (Figure 35 below), are difficult to control with a capturing or an inadequately designed receiving hood. Energised dust clouds will normally require a partial enclosure or a well-designed receiving hood into which the cloud can be directed; from the hood receptacle, the dust cloud should quickly be directed into the extracting LEV duct. Otherwise, the hood will become saturated with dust, reducing the efficacy of the receiving hood.

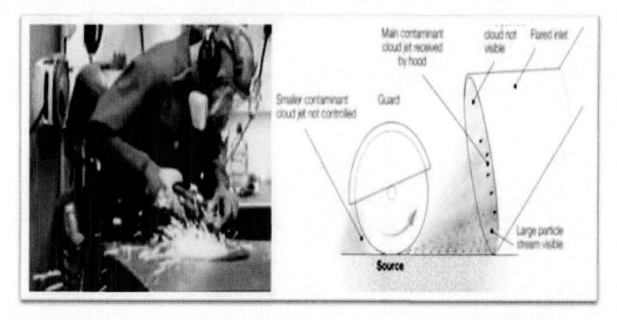

Figure 35[127] On the left hand side, a grinding operation is showing energetic particles being projected into a large area. A receiving hood on the right is not good enough to capture all the fine particles. A small portion of the fine contaminant cloud jet, as marked in the Figure, is not controlled by the receiving hood because this portion is not being propelled in the direction of the receiving hood. For this reason, this work activity using the control as shown would require the

use of suitable, sufficient and correctly worn RPE. Alternatively, a partially enclosing hood may be used.

Examples of receiving hoods are shown later in Figure 40. Other examples were shown earlier in Figures 21 and 26 in Chapter 4. In summary, work activity energised contaminant clouds could be propelled into receiving hoods by the energetic movement of the process-induced SHH/air (Figure above). The hood and its face must be big enough to receive the energetic contaminant cloud. The extraction system's air must take away the contaminant in the hood as fast as it is filled/received.

5.6 Vapour is heavier than air, misconception

There are workplace situations where LEV can be designed and used for removing solvent vapours, including those heavier than air (e.g. dichloromethane, phenol). Even when the vapour is heavier than air (vapour density), in normal work activities, only a small amount of vapour mixed in air sinks towards the floor. This is due to cloud density, air currents and mixing/whirling effects. A significant portion of the vapour rises upwards, as well as moves sideways, as illustrated in the **reality** diagram in Figure 36.

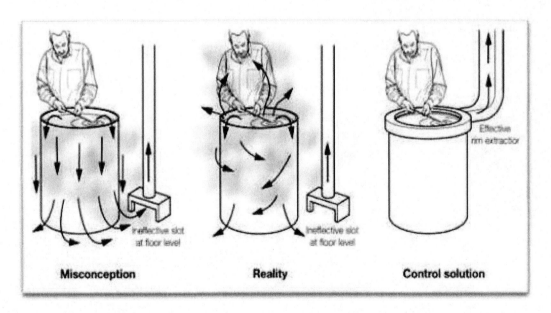

Figure 36[127] Different approaches for controlling exposure to solvent vapour.

Misconception: not recognising the reality, resulting in an ineffective ventilation hood design placed at floor level. **Reality:** in this situation, the hood's capture zone (bubble) isn't close to the source (and the working zone) to extract the pollutant away from the BZ of the operator. **Control solution:** as an example, a rim hood extraction is shown. It should be effective so long as: (i) the extraction rim is of the right configuration and size to fit the solvent tank snugly; (ii) the tank is filled to an appropriate design-determined depth to allow sufficient headspace to cope with wake and draught effects; (iii) LEV is correctly used; and (iv) LEV testing, checking and maintenance are in place. Additional benefits of the control solution design include saving on energy costs, reducing excessive vapour discharge to the outside atmosphere (green chemistry) and a reduced need for RPE.

5.7 Missing importance sources of exposure

Figure 37 shows a common control problem. In this case, extraction is provided for dust control during sack unloading, but uncontrolled 'empty' sack disposal. In addition, the LEV hood system shown in Figure 37 lacks a ledge to support/rest sacks, creating a situation for dust escape during tipping. These exposure control scenarios (emptying and disposing of empty sacks) show that RM measures for associated activities in a process should be considered together rather than as task-by-task RAs and RM control measures. A "total risk concept" is necessary to achieve proportionate, harm-based risk control. This principle is enshrined in the requirement of the COSHH good control practice principle as "Ensure that the introduction of control measures does not increase the overall risk to health and safety". This is where HSE's risk assessment template becomes useful (Section 4.16).

Figure 37[127] LEV design missing important contaminant exposure sources.

OSHKE

Figure 37 and the design of the hood:

1. This design is without a suitable ledge, presenting a potential for dust exposure. How? *Please reflect on contributory factors, and don't miss product spills and coverall contamination.*

2.   With this control design, is there a potential for issues related to muscular skeletal strain to the operators? *Yes*

3.   What would happen to dust exposure when the 'empty' bags are compressed? – Observe the figure, c*an you see a light grey dust cloud being expelled, creating a potential for inhalation and skin exposure, and for the contamination of surfaces, including PPE. What about inadvertent ingestion exposure (skin to mouth)?*

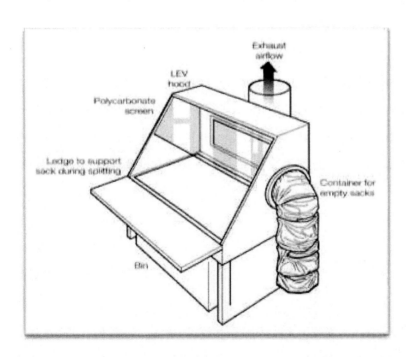

Figure 38[127] An improved design is shown, when compared with the one in Figure 37.

This design takes account of manual handling, the potential for product spillage during product loading, a deep enclosure face to minimise effects from eddies, a facility for immediate disposal of empty bags and for easy waste disposal of empty sacks later.

A number of other simple, cost-effective nudges could be designed in by the designer of the system to further improve efficacy – e.g. LED light (red/green) when the empty sacks container is in/out of its round seating socket. What else: Stacking/lifting facility for handling unopened sacks with products.

5.8 Operator standing in the wrong place

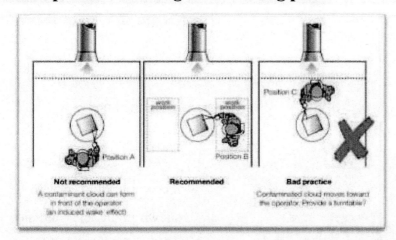

Figure 39[127] Walk-in spray booth and sprayer positions (a top view).

Looking at the **'Not recommended'** and the **'Bad practice'** in Figure 39, have you ever observed practices like those shown by positions A and C? Don't be surprised. It is a common problem in walk-in booths like the design shown.

Recommended is a simple solution. Further, nudging approaches could be included: a manually operated turn table and marking the "working positions" on the floor. These will go a long way for significantly reducing the exposure to SHH, like isocyanates, epoxy resins, paint sprays, powder coatings, and solvent-vapours. A mechanised turn table with a foot-pedal operation is even better. You need to think about intrinsic safety issues when an electrical motor is used for mechanisation in a spray booth. For dealing with awkward shaped items like cars, down draught walk-in booths are ideal.

OSHKE

What do you think about the suggested nudging approaches? More information on nudging is in chapter 11.

5.9 Head in contaminated air

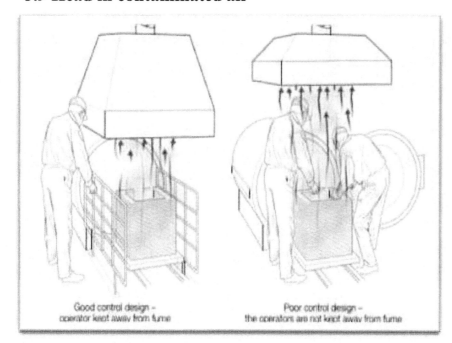

Good control design – operator kept away from fume

Poor control design – the operators are not kept away from fume

Figure 40[127] Good and poor designs of exposure control, including LEV receiving hoods.

A 'good control' receiving hood design is shown in the left hand side of Figure 40. It has a better designed hood configuration compared to the 'poor control design' on the right. The barriers are automatic opt-ins. These barriers act as positive nudges for exposure control and keeping the operator's head/BZ away from fume. How many times have you observed the "head in contaminated air" situation and the related LEV hood design? Don't let it happen in your watch. 'Head in contaminated air' hood designs are commonly seen in welding bays and foundries.

OSHKE

With reference to Figure 40: If the fume is a respiratory sensitiser and/or carcinogen and the work is done 3-shifts a day, 5-days a week, what other proportionate controls could be added to the good control design shown to reduce exposure as low as is reasonably practicable? *For example: (i) an inexpensive barrier break detection; (ii) an alarm linked to fume levels; (iii) oven door lock release associated with fume clearance time concentration (at a pre-set level) inside the barrel shaped oven.*

However, control options, their design and installation will be influenced by, among other things, production rate/temperature, the ways products are handled, product flow during the process, the operatives work practices and the organisational environment.

5.10 One size hood fit for all

Figure 41[130] The operator is handling solvent soaked fabric coating material (rubber-dough). Two one sized hoods are at the background.

Figure 41 shows two ineffective captor hoods for controlling solvent vapour. These hoods are sited well outside the working zone of the operator. One of the hoods is well away from the open face of the shiny metal bucket containing solvent soaked rubber dough and the red solvent dispensing can. (Allow for an optical illusion when looking at the picture). The other hood is well away from the operator's hand holding the dough.

The operator would carry the "ball shaped" dough in his unprotected hands (after he has formed the ball using his bare hands) and place it in front of the "dough spreading-knife" of a fabric coating machine (not shown). During his working day, he would use the solvent in the red container to help remove residual dough that had stuck to his skin and to make the dough softer for handling. An alternative option for hands-free dough dispensing is shown in Figure 42.

OSHKE

Figure 41, some questions.

(i) Taking account of what you see in the Figure, do you consider that the employer would have undertaken a suitable and sufficient RA? *No, explore the obvious reasons using visual observations. Is the operator using his coverall as a source for wiping his hands?*

(ii) Who would have recommended and designed the LEV system as installed? *Most likely by incompetent persons.*

(iii) Who would have installed the LEV system? *Most likely by an incompetent person who did not understand work flow/practices.*

(iv) Do you think that the designer and the installer would have spoken to the people doing the work? *Most unlikely.*

(v) Do you think that the designer and the installer would have understood, taken note and catered for the nitty-gritty of the work activities/practices and their effects on operator exposure? *Most unlikely.*

(vi) Based on the design, do you think that the designer and the installer would have been CPs? *See above.*

(vii) How did they get away with this poor design and its installation which would have resulted in unacceptable expenditure? *Many theories, including a short-term fix that became a permanent solution, A salesperson overselling the capability of the one size hood fits all situations. The operator has just a pair of hands, how could we expect him to do the job and constantly pull and push the elephant trunk ducting.*

(viii) What could be said about the LEV fourteen monthly tester? *Most likely to be an incompetent person or the application of the person's professional code of conduct to this job is questionable.*

(ix) Assuming that the employer had the services of an in-house OSH officer and a Group OSH Manager, why did things go wrong and is it to do with operating beyond their competency envelope? *Many theories.*

(x) Would you provide or recommend a pump action solvent dispenser for cleaning hands, (for that matter using a solvent for cleaning hands)? *No.*

(xi) Is it acceptable to do the dough-ball forming job wearing suitable gloves? *If the job is done repeatedly and throughout the working day, and day after day, not enough would be done to comply with good practice requirements. It is proportional to use semi-automation. If the job is a short run on the day, requiring dough handling for a limited time, then a correct gloves option could be considered.*

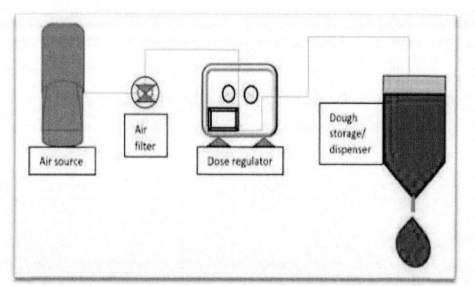

Figure 42: A sketch showing a potential hands-free dough dispensing arrangement.

5.11 Substance is not classified as hazardous by the GHS system, no need for LEV

Some substances used at work may not be classified under the GHS system. However, in use they can create inhalable dust and they may have assigned WELs as well as be subjected to the current HSE advice on dust trigger values as explained in Chapter 1. The dusty substance, used in the process shown in Figure 43, is a SHH because WELs has been assigned and it falls within the requirements of good practice control. To some extent, the employer has recognised the issue and provided RPE.

Figure 43[130] A dusty work activity and inadequate exposure control. It shows a cable is being coated with a white anti-stick powder and then being wound into a reel. This activity is being undertaken without suitable at the source-exposure control measures.

Also note, (i) the respirator wearer has not used the bottom strap of the respirator (it was tucked inside the mask, only a single strap was used and the mask is not fitted correctly); (ii) dust is seen on the floor and on many areas of the turntable. Inhalable size dust in the air is very difficult to see with the naked eyes and without supplementary lighting. A practical demonstration can be seen at a demonstration of a dust lamp[175]. In this YouTube film, note the way a captor hood has been converted to improve efficacy. You may also look at the pictures in HSE dust lamp guidance[176].

OSHKE

Figure 43, some questions.

1.   Do you need to carry out BZ air monitoring/sampling or health surveillance to conclude that "good practice" is not in force and the exposure is not being adequately controlled? *No.*

2.   You will note that the COSHH regulations 10 on exposure monitoring is qualified by "where the risk assessment indicates". In this case, a 'walk-through' survey should conclude: exposure control measures are inadequate and that the measures required for achieving and maintaining adequate control are x, y, and z.

3.   Do you consider that by providing health surveillance to this worker, compliance with COSHH can be mitigated to a large extent? *If the answer is yes, most definitely a false assumption. Regulations 11 on health surveillance is qualified by "where it is appropriate". In this case employer's priority should be on establishing adequate exposure control and making sure suitable and sufficient RPE is used correctly as a temporary measure. Use these carefully crafted regulatory tools (COSHH regulations 10 and 11) judicially to (i) help achieve adequate exposure control; (ii) to minimise unnecessary and unhelpful expenditure, paper work, records keeping; and (iii) minimise opportunities for creating disclosure requirements to workers, trade unions, HSE inspectors etc.*

4.   Do you agree that, in this case, some help from a competent occupational hygienist/exposure control design engineer and/or a surface coating specialist would be beneficial for getting advice on designing exposure control to dust? *Yes.*

5.12 Barbecue smoke effect

Barbecue smoke effect is created by swirling (eddies) air, (Figure 44). This type of effect can be created at the entrance of a fume cupboard, other partial enclosures, booths, air islands and at the air outlets of LEV discharge points, as seen in Figure 44. To minimise the effects of a swirling air cloud at the entrance of a hood (several visual examples are illustrated in HS258[127]), hood designers should take account of the effect and users should be trained and instructed to use the hood/enclosure correctly.

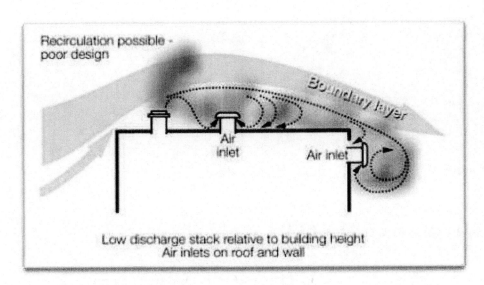

Figure 44[127] Effects of swirling air is illustrated.

To avoid extracted discharged air re-entering the building, precautions can be put in place, such as:

- Discharged air must leave the discharge duct at a high enough speed to make sure it is dispersed well away from the boundaries of the building. It can be achieved by putting a tapered nozzle on the outlet or a slight bend (illustrations in (b) of Figure 45, below). Never accept the capping approach shown in Figure 45 below. The illustration shows what can happen to the discharged contaminant.
- The discharge point should be located well above the highest point of the building.
- The designer should know about the airflow patterns around a new installation.
- The designer should take into account of air inlets associated with the building where LEV is involved.

So, every time a hood, enclosure or air discharge point is designed, you need to ask the designer, how will they prevent or minimise the effects arising from swirling air.

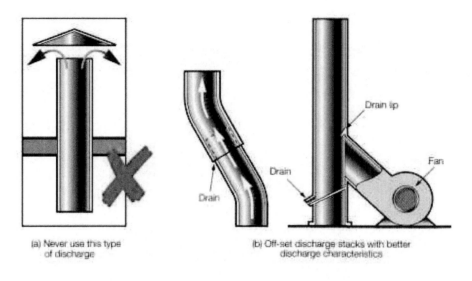

(a) Never use this type of discharge

(b) Off-set discharge stacks with better discharge characteristics

Figure 45[127] illustrations showing stack design.

5.13 Working in the open air, no need for LEV

Figure 46[130] A DIY stone cutting at a construction site.

An observation of the Figure will show that the activity could be taking place for a considerable period. The work is being undertaken without suitable exposure control measures, including manual handling tasks. Dust containing respirable crystalline silica can settle on clothing. There is a real potential for third party exposure, for example, other workers at the site, people at the operator's home and co-workers/public sitting close to this operator whilst travelling. Think about this operative and another two being seated on the front seats of a work-van. Looking at the Figure, there could be a significant potential for contamination of the electrical systems. The DIY workbench is being used as a clothing store.

Figure 46, a few questions.

(i) If a contract work person carried out this work at your site, what types of positive nudges will you put in their way, rather than throwing the OSH law at them? *What about using the contract documentation requiring extracted cutting equipment attached to an industrial vacuum cleaner.*

(ii) Make a close observation of the picture and identify potential activities leading to hazardous manual handling tasks.

(iii) Will any of the manual handling activities further exacerbate inhalation exposure to dust? *Yes.*

(iv) In this example, reflect on safety issues and your thoughts on implementing task-based RA using HSE's RA template *(Section 4.16).*

(vi)   How would you minimise the potential risks arising from the manual handling of bricks?

For dust control approaches: Controlling construction dust with on-tool extraction CIS69 (hse.gov.uk) and for manual handling related issues: Blocks and masonry units - Specific tasks - Manual handling - Controlling physical health risks - Managing occupational health risks in construction (hse.gov.uk)

5.14 General ventilation

General ventilation is about reducing the concentration of SHH in work air by introducing uncontaminated air into the workroom atmosphere and causing the 'fresh' air to mix with SHH contaminated air, before moving the mixed air out of the workroom. This can be achieved by forced dilution or using the natural flow of air through open air grilles, windows, doors etc.

In forced dilution ventilation, the contaminant is mixed with fresh air blown in as shown in Figure 47 below. The Illustrations on the left show that the air flow pattern is taking place in such a way that the diluted contaminated air is taken away through the BZs of workers. These types of design arrangements are all too common in many workplaces. However, they can be easily avoided as illustrated in the right hand side illustrations of Figure 47.

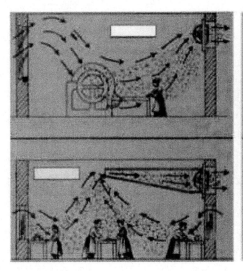 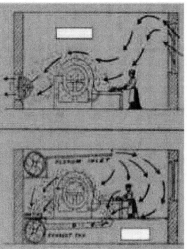

Figure 47[12] Illustrations showing approaches used in forced dilution ventilation designs.

OSHKE

What are the key design arrangements that are helpful in the correct design of the general mechanical ventilation systems shown in Figure 47 *Location of the fan is helping air exit and the grilles are helping good air movement around the operator. Plenum is used for supplying air. However, recall about the effects of eddies. So, to achieve adequate exposure control, 'at source' control should be the preferred option. These types of general ventilation systems may have been used widely in operating theatres of the 80s. Today, at source, active/passive scavenging systems are in common use.*

5.15 A list of examples of problems associated with incorrect LEV operation

1. Ineffective hood	2. Failure to maintain adequate transport velocity in the ducting.
3. Movable extraction hoods incorrectly positioned	4. Making the original fit for purpose LEV system ineffective over time. For example, by adding additional extraction hoods without appropriate design changes
5. Hoods incorrectly installed	6. 'Head in the contaminated air'
7. Working outside the capture zone of a captor hood	8. Barbecue effect at the hood face areas and at the LEV discharge point/building air intakes
9. Damaged extraction hood	10. Incorrectly designed discharge outlet
11. Holes in extraction hoods and ducting	12. Walk-in booths, operator standing in the contaminant transport flow

13. Failing to establish the capture zone/capture velocity needed for effective capture of contaminants	14. When using recirculating LEV, failing to ensure returned air quality
15. Not taking initiatives to visually indicate the capture zones of hoods	16. Incorporating rectangular ducts over a long distance of the ducting system
17. Using one size hood as a fit for all extraction needs	18. Ducting not secured/anchored causing leaks and other problems
19. Contaminant leakage/seepage through joints and baffles in LEV systems	20. Installing movable extraction hoods which are heavy/difficult for manual positioning
21. Incorrect assumptions when designing hoods and ducting	22. An ineffective design for safe removal of used dustbag and for fitting new ones
23. When using recirculating LEV, failing to act on the air quality information	24. Hoods not appropriate for the work practices
25. When using recirculating/nonrecirculating LEV, failure to consider or design-in suitable makeup air facility	26. Fume cupboard sash opening mechanisms without user friendly indicators (mechanical or visual types)
27. Blocked filters on nonrecirculating systems	28. Incorrectly designed air islands
29. Blocked filters on recirculating systems	30. Damaged doors and seals in booths
31. Too many 90-degree bends in ducting systems	32. Down draught floor outlet damaged or partially blocked
33. Obstruction within the ducting systems, such as solidified/caked up deposits caused by poor duct design or inadequate transport velocity or a combination of both	34. Water wash systems not maintained

5.16 Summary

Extraction ventilation and to some extent, general ventilation, is one of the common ways to minimise excessive exposure to SHH. For the systems to be effective, they should be properly conceptualised, designed, installed, maintained and used. Unfortunately, this may not happen in all workplaces. In this Chapter and in the previous one, examples of poor design, installation and use have been presented to explain some of the problems and how they could be avoided. In a vast majority of cases, design, installation and maintenance are a job for competent people. COSHH Essential direct advice sheets[92], the buying and using LEV guide[170] and the films referenced in this chapter are essential resources for OSH practitioners. You should actively cultivate the culture for achieving adequate exposure control through correctly designed LEV and where appropriate using the right types of general ventilation. Examples in this book should help you to make a difference.

Chapter 6 Respiratory Protective Equipment (RPE) and COSHH Risk Management

"The quality of airs, waters, and places to which people are exposed, are important to the health of individuals."
- *Hippocrates, The father of Medicine.*

6.1 Introduction

Before being placed on the market, RPE design, its manufacture and conformity with approved standards are subjected to a high degree of testing and quality assurance. These requirements should be met before relevant conformity marking is placed on RPE (unless illegally supplied to the marketplace). RPE is classified into two main types – filtering respirators and breathing apparatus (BA).

In many workplaces, RPE is used as one of the important exposure control measures against excessive inhalation exposure to SHH. However, there have been avoidable exposures, serious accidents and fatalities due to incorrect selection and/or misuse of RPE. Areas of failure include a dirty dozen:

o As with the selection and use of LEV, a lack of knowledge about the physical and chemical properties of SHH and their likely concentration levels in the air.
o Incorrect selection of a respirator type.
o Using unsuitable respirator filters for protection against SHH.
o Selecting RPE with insufficient protection levels, known as assigned protection factors (APF) against airborne concentration levels.
o Incorrect use of RPE including failing to undertake fit testing for tight fitting face pieces.
o Using respirators in confined spaces (CS).
o Incorrect donning.
o Supplying poor quality compressed air to BA.
o A lack of schedule maintenance of reusable RPE.
o DIY repairs.
o Incorrect storage.
o Misuse of RPE.

111

These easily avoidable common failures are never acceptable or tolerable after thirty years of COSHH. Incorrect selection and use, including misuse, and lack of maintenance, invalidate the RPE adequacy and suitability requirements of the law. Similarly, buying an RPE, for that matter any PPE, which is not in compliance (illegal products) with the PPE regulations, can seriously compromise the OSH of the wearers, put employers against the law, and weakens the British legitimate industry which invests considerable resources to obtain conformity certification.

OSHKE

If you are involved in RPE selection:

1.   Do you know, how to interpret the conformity markings on RPE and its components such as filters, face pieces etc.? *If you are not sure, contact the* British Safety Industry Federation (BSIF).

2.   Do you know how to check for illegally supplied RPE? *If you are not sure, contact BSIF.*

At face value, it might seem easy to select the right RPE for a given situation and SHH. However, it is important to note that for many workplace situations, it will require some, at times extensive, involvement of competent people because several delicately balanced factors must be considered and actions must be taken to enable correct selection and safe use. In this Chapter, many of these issues are explored to help you, and your operations colleagues for providing adequate protection for the workforce, comply with the law and reap a better RoI.

There are plenty of free-to-use and pay-to-use training resources on RPE. Free-to-use materials include, 'Health Risks at Work! Do You Know Yours?'[145], LOcHER-RPE[177], the 'Clean Air? Take Care!'[178] and the RPE selector tool[179].

6.2 RPE selection

To select the right RPE, you will have to take into account the properties of the SHH against which protection is required; the needs of the wearer; the needs of the work; and the conditions of the work environment. This is pictorially summarised in Figure 48.

Figure 48[178] A summary of key RPE selection factors.

An introduction to RPE selection, its use and maintenance can be found in HSE guidance HSG53[180]. A step-by-step approach for deciding the minimum level of protection - known as assigned protection factor or APF - that will be needed for a work activity involving a SHH, along with associated selection factors, can be found in the RPE selector tool[179]. It was developed by the Scottish Healthy Working Lives in partnership with HSE and supported by professional/trade organisations. This selector tool is based on the principles of the COSHH-Essentials Control Banding approach[94], but takes one more step forward to include process generated substances, gases, fumes and products containing solids and solvents. To use it, you don't need expert knowledge in RPE, but you should have correct information on RPE selection factors. They are summarised in Figure 49. However, when using the selector tool, several checks and balances questions with their benchmarks will guide you through a stepwise journey. By getting familiar with the selector tool, you can very quickly become an expert in using it.

The output from the tool is like an NHS prescription form prescribed by your medical practitioner. After you tell them your health issues and them asking you questions, you get a prescription form to give to a dispensing chemist, who may ask confirmatory questions, such as name, before handing over the medicine. So, once you show the output from the selector tool to a BSIF Registered RPE safety supplier, they can work out the right RPE. They may ask clarifying questions to ensure that the RPE they dispense is the right one. As a norm, BSIF registered RPE suppliers go through training on dispensing RPE. However, you may use other approaches, but make sure they are good enough in quality and will support you to make the right decisions.

Company name	BR4YOU		
Task need RPE	Spray painting galvanised cones		
Work area - high risks	Confined space: No	Oxygen deficient: No	Flammable: No
Substance in use:	xylene, trimethylbenzenes (isomers), pigments and fillers		
Other PPE:	Safety goggles		
Control measures used:	partially enclosing booth, manually operated turn table, operator position marked		
Substance hazard data:	COSHH Essentials Health Hazard Group: C	Amount in use: Medium	Physical state: Mist, solvent-based (or solid in solvent)
Task duration (total): 04:00	Amount of time RPE is worn continuously for without taking a break or finishing the task: More than 1 hour	Work rate - effort needed: Medium	Precise communication needed: No
Assigned protection factor (HSE/HSG53):	20 or higher.		
Recommended filter and/or class of RPE:	Type combination A1P3, or breathing apparatus (BA).		
RPE types for which fit testing is needed: 4, 7, 8		RPE types for which NO fit testing is needed: 5, 9	
Notes:	For solvents with BP<65C, use AX. AX Single use only		
Assessor's name:	Bob Rajan		
Assessment date:	26/09/2021		

Quick Links

Facemask fit testing information

Recommended masks

- 4. Fan-powered reusable full-face mask respirator
- 5. Fan-powered respirator with reusable hood, helmet or visor
- 7. Compressed airline breathing apparatus (CABA) with half mask
- 8. CABA or powered FAHBA with full face-mask
- 9. CABA or powered FAHBA with hood, helmet or visor

Figure 49[179] An example recommendation output from the RPE selector tool.

6.3 Incorrect selection of RPE

Table 13 below provides examples of incorrect selection. To avoid these problems, consider using the RPE selector tool[179] introduced in 6.2 or an equivalent systematic approach. Otherwise, seek the advice of a CP.

Table 13 Examples of incorrect selection of RPE.

Commonly found incorrect/ineffective RPE use	Reasons
Wear compatibility	Tight fitting face pieces and facial hair in the face seal region.
	Tight fitting face pieces issued without wearer/mask agreement. Failing to undertake face piece fit testing.
	Mask clashing with goggles, spectacles and hearing protectors.
	Side arms of spectacles interfering with adequacy of face seal.
	Mask straps worn on top of head covering/hood. It can affect the face seal due to moving/shifting head covering/straps.
Incorrect/misuse	Fit tested tightfitting face piece worn when hair is present in the face seal area.
	Lower strap of disposable mask left hanging or tucked inside the mask. All straps on tight fitting masks should be secured well to get an adequate seal.
	Mask straps worn incorrectly, causing problems for the efficacy of face seal.
	Disposable masks worn upside down.
	Nose bridge on disposable half masks not adjusted properly.

	Book like foldable disposable masks - designed for cost reduction, ease of packaging which supports green chemistry (reduced packaging waste, reduced storage and transport spaces) - worn without unfolding the mask.
	Wearing mask below the nose.
	Disposable respirators stored in a helmet webbing or in pockets and in crushed form.
Maintenance and cleaning	Wearing a reusable respirator with damaged valve seating. If the exhalation valve is damaged, contaminants can enter easily through the damage.
	Hair, layers of dust and other dirt on valve seating; perished valves. These can cause incorrect valve operation and help contaminant inward leakage (by passing the filter, due to less flow resistance).
	Damaged components like O-rings, cracked visors, out of date filters, deformed/crushed masks, DIY repairs, and using solvents to clean masks.
	On power assisted RPE: inadequately charged batteries, battery compartment seals and connections damaged. Breathing (air supply) hose not connected correctly and inadequate air flow. DIY repairs of batteries and breathing hoses.
Training	RPE users/supervisors not receiving adequate training and instruction.
Supervision	Tight fitting RPE is very uncomfortable to wear, especially for a long time. Wearers need motivation and supervision to get through hassle factors. Unpowered respirators are uncomfortable to wear continuously for more than an hour and during high work rates. Alternatives should be provided.
RPE without communication devices	In 'safety' critical operations, face piece should not cause communication difficulties. Suitable devices should be used.

6.4 Examples of other issues with RPE use

Table 14 provides examples of commonly found ineffective uses of RPE. These issues will affect performance and the extent of protection. You should look out for these when RPE is used at your workplace and take measures to eradicate the problems.

Table 14 Examples of incorrect selection

Work activity - examples	Type of RPE used	Why is it an incorrect selection
Mineral wool laying in lofts.	Doubled up nuisance dust mask (NDM) – Figure 50.	NDMs are NOT designed/certified/conformity marked for use against SHH. That is why they are called NDMs.
Spray painting including isocyanates based.	NDMs.	See above.
Handling grain dust, wood dust or other types.	NDMs. Sometimes FFP1 (Filtering Face piece with P1 filter)	Explanation in first row. For wood/silica dust, FFP3 should be worn to reduce exposure as low as is reasonably practical. A P1 filter has low filtration efficiency, ~ 80-85%; P2, ~ 90% and P3, ~ 99.9%.
Welding fume.	FFP1, FFP2 or NDM.	HSE recommends protection level/APF of at least 20, along with other at source control measures. Welding fume is a carcinogen, exposure should be reduced as low as is reasonably practical.
Work involving organic solvent-based products (e.g. painting, cleaning, degreasing, printing, glass reinforced plastics manufacture, repair etc.	NDM or particle respirators with P1, P2 or P3 filters.	NDMs, see rows above. Particle filters do not trap solvent vapours. RPE selector tool could be used, providing all relevant information has been input to the tool.

Entering a ship hold to do work or rescue someone in danger.	P3 type filtering respirator.	Respirators are unsuitable for entering a CS with oxygen deficiency. Suitable BA must be worn, as part of a safe working system which complies with Confined Spaces (CS) Regulations.
Work with refrigerant gas - ammonia.	Type 'A' organic vapour filter.	Organic vapour filters are inappropriate. Suitable and adequate 'K' type filters needed, taking account of other selection factors (Figure 48), use and maintenance matters.
Work involving acetone or dichloromethane (DCM).	Type 'A' organic vapour filter.	Type 'A' filters are designed for solvents with boiling points above 65C. Acetone and DCM have lower boiling points and require suitable 'AX' type filters specifically recommended by the manufacture/RPE supplier.
Entering a drained and cleaned degreasing tank which previously contained an organic solvent.	Full-face mask with 'A1' filter.	Even though the tank may appear to be fully drained of solvent and cleaned. There is always a potential for some residual (may be a few millilitres) solvent/sludge in the tank. This can produce a lot of vapour very quickly. The vapours produced by the residual solvent can make the tank a CS, making it an oxygen deficient atmosphere and full of vapour cloud. Suitable BA should be used. There were many fatalities associated with CS working and incorrect RPE use.
Using diesel powered power breakers in restricted or CSs.	FFP2 respirator.	Diesel machines can produce significant amount of colourless, odourless life threating carbon monoxide (CO) gas, as well as carbon dioxide and diesel engine exhaust fume. The activity also creates dust. So, protection is needed against oxygen deficiency, CO, fume and dust. A suitable BA is the answer. There were many CO related fatalities.

  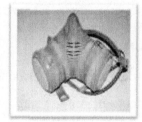

Figure 50[181]Examples of incorrectly selected, used and/or maintained RPE (set A)

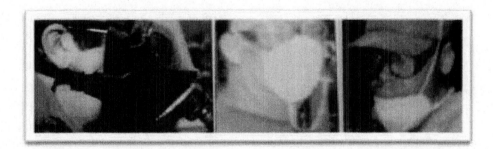

Figure 51[181] Examples of incorrectly used RPE (set B)

119

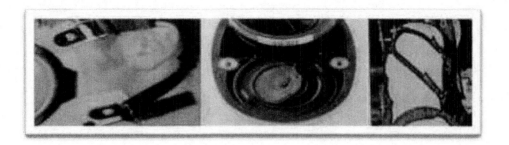

Figure 52[181] Examples of incorrectly used/maintained RPE (set C)

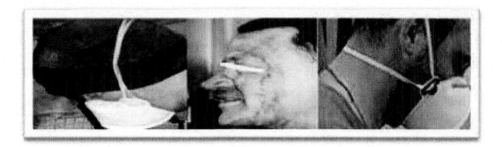

Figure 53[181] Examples of incorrectly used RPE/situation (set D)

6.5 Summary

RPE is widely used in workplaces for providing protection against airborne SHH. However, incorrect selection, misuse and inadequate maintenance are major barriers preventing the effective use of RPE. OSH practitioners should deploy appropriate efforts to eradicate these problems. Examples in this Chapter should help you.

Appendix 6.1 Explanation to RPE pictures in Figures 50, 51, 52 and 53.

In each case, explore the reason for the state of affair, remembering that human errors cannot be parked on employees only.

RPE pictures	Explanation
Figure 50	**Left hand side picture:** *Doubled up NDMs used for protection against SHH in the belief that doubling up will be good enough for protection. This is an incorrect selection and misuse of NDMs which are not RPE under regulatory requirements (find out).* **Picture in the middle:** *A badly damaged/scratched face visor on a full-face mask. It will curtail visibility, provide a potential for lifting the mask when in a contaminated area; presents a potential for accidents involving slips and trips. The damage may have been due to energetic particles (such as those created in shot blasting activities) impacting on the visor. Peelable visors available.* **Right hand side picture:** *A heavily contaminated half mask, suggesting RPE on its own is unlikely to provide adequate protection. It is hoped that this RPE didn't form part of the RA for the task. The situation could present a significant potential for clogging of filters, damage to valve seating and inadequate APF. The wearer will attempt to lift the mask to make life comfortable, leading to exposure. This contaminated mask presents a significant potential for skin contamination.*
Figure 51	**Left hand side picture:** *Ordinary side-arm spectacles worn with a full face mask, creating a potential for poor face seal and inward leakage of airborne SHH.* **Picture in the middle:** *A filtering face piece RPE worn using top strap only. There is a clash between the mask and the spectacles creating a poor seal in the top part of the mask. Fitted upside down.* **Right hand side picture:** *A filtering face piece worn incorrectly, straps worn over the head gear, limiting the extent of protection for the wearer. Anyhow, the wearer has not fitted the mask correctly. One of the reasons could be that the RPE was unsuitable for the task, which may have been undertaken over several hours of the working day. Work rate involved may be creating a high breathing rate and correctly wearing the RPE could cause discomfort to the wearer. It is possible that the wearer was not involved in RPE selection. Nose bridge clip has not been pinched to shape the mask. A further*

	dissection will lead to uncovering many more issues with selection and use of RPE. A HSE inspector, if they wanted, could spend hours at the worksite and submit a hefty 'fees for intervention' invoice. You and I know HSE is a progressive minded organisation and therefore, it is most likely that an Improvement Notice citing relevant aspects of HSW Act and COSHH regulations would be used very quickly, resulting in a cost and resource efficient fees for intervention invoice.
Figure 52	**Lefthand side picture:** *one of the head harnesses on this full face mask has not been tightened, creating the potential for inward leakage of SHH. The mask can slip on the face during work. An expensive RPE used ineffectively.* **Picture in the middle:** *A perished exhalation vale on a half mask respirator. Explore the effect on protection caused by a perished exhalation valve. Examples like, a badly contaminated seating in the exhalation valve seal area, hair strands in between the valve and its seating area can lead to poor protection against SHH.* **Right hand side picture:** *A full face mask harness straps worn over the headgear of a coverall. What will be the effect on protection, when the headgear is subjected to pull and slack during a work activity? The way the PPE (coverall and RPE) is worn, what will be the effect on the comfort factors for the wearer? What reasons could have contributed to the situation?*
Figure 53	**Left hand side picture:** Mask straps twisted together to make one; *Incorrect wearing reduces protection. Examine the potential reasons that would have led to this situation – include in your examination, RPE selection factors, training, management, supervision and competency of the employer.* **Picture in the middle:** *Signs of contaminant inward leakage due to poor face seal. Is there a requirement in the COSHH ACoP - select tight fitting masks by fit testing. What types of fit testing methods are available? Which organisation is involved in certifying the competency levels of fit testers.* **Right hand side picture:** *A disposable mask worn with hair in the face seal area. What are the consequences of this situation for protecting the wearer from exposure to SHH.*

Chapter 7: Skin Exposure to Substances Hazardous to Health and Its Control

"Traditional wisdom, as demonstrated by myriads of Material Safety Data Sheets, suggests that decontaminating the skin should be a simple phenomenon: simply rinse with soap and water. Today, we realise this traditional wisdom not only lacks an experimental basis, but is often wrong."

- *Professor Howard I Maibach, Dermatologist and scientist.*

7.1 Skin Exposure at work

Skin exposure to manufactured chemical substances/products and process-generated substances encountered at work can affect the skin of operatives or can pass through their skin and cause diseases elsewhere in the body. Helped by the improvements in 'at source' control measures and the availability and use of skin protection measures - good quality PPE, skin protection creams and good standards of welfare facilities - work-related skin diseases have been falling over the years (Figure 4 in Chapter 1). A little more effort, however, could make it better for all workers, in particular florists, beauticians, cooks, hairdressers, barbers, construction workers and certain manufacturing and health-care-related workers. To work towards this aim, some key aspects associated with skin exposure and its control are discussed in sections below. Additional information and advice can be found in HSE's 'skin at work' web pages[182].

7.2 Dynamics of skin exposure

The **process of transferring contamination to the skin** is somewhat different from inhalation exposure because contaminants may move rapidly to and from the skin. In other words, the transfer process **is multidirectional and dynamic**, which is explored using Figure 54 below.

Figure 54[130] Dynamics of skin exposure is explained using a dust-contaminated coverall.

The picture in Figure 54 was taken with the help of a Tyndall lamp technique[175,176] to illuminate fine dust particles in the air and make them visible. As seen in Figure 54, dust deposited on the coverall is released from it by the action of the hands touching the contaminated coverall. It resulted in recontamination of the air close to the BZ of the person. The aerosolised dust, in turn, creates a potential for inhalation exposure. In addition, some of the aerosolised dust may return to the coverall and inner clothing, other parts of the skin and may settle on surfaces close by. The contaminated hands can potentially transfer the contamination to the skin on the face and can create a potential for inadvertent ingestion exposure. Dust settled on surfaces can re-enter the air and settle for the second time on the skin.

Work-related inadvertent ingestion exposure is caused by contact between the mouth and contaminated hands and objects. In general, exposed individuals may be unaware of the potential for and the occurrence of inadvertent exposure. It can be a significant source of excessive exposure to highly toxic SHH. So, OSH practitioners should pay attention to reducing skin contamination, improving the cleanness of workplaces and reduction in the contamination of work equipment, in situations where inadvertent exposure can be a significant route of exposure. A further discussion and visual examples of dermal exposure pathways can be seen in Section 7.3.

OSHKE

1. With reference to Figure 54, do you consider that the dust created by the originating activity had been adequately controlled? *Not at all.*

2. Do you consider that the activity would have complied with the good practice requirements, including the need to minimise the emission, release and spread of SHH. *No.*

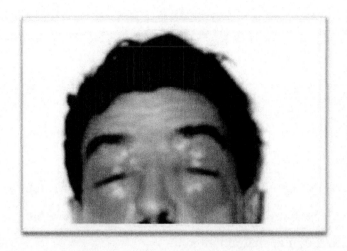

Figure 55[130] Skin allergy caused by exposure to skin sensitising epoxy resin. Many accelerators used in epoxy resins carry H317 health hazard statement – it may cause an allergic skin reaction.

This Figure shows a person suffering from an allergic reaction caused by exposure to epoxy resin. It happened due to contaminated dust in the air depositing on the skin and the contaminated hands regularly touching the face.

Figure 56[130] Solvents and printing inks - contamination transfer from gloves (PPE) and a contaminated rag (a surface).

Solvents and inks are widely used in the printing industry. Figure 56 shows the surface contamination of a glove. This glove and the cleaning rag can act as sources for transferring contamination onto work surfaces. From there, the transfer can take place to other nearby sources to create the potential for skin contamination as well as inhalation exposure to solvent vapours.

OSHKE

1. Looking at the contamination levels on the glove surfaces (Figure 56), do you consider that an <u>adequate</u> safe working distance (SWD) approach was in operation? *No, it could be that the employer and the operatives had a misconstrued view that skin exposure to solvents and dyes is part and parcel of the job and using gloves will help to reduce the problem.*

2. Can you think of SWD tools that could be used in this situation? *What about a tool with a short handle? What about process redesign or modification to improve work practices.*

7.3 Skin exposure pathways

To devise suitable and effective dermal exposure control measures, it is necessary to be familiar with skin exposure pathways. These are:

Immersion *(hands)* - Skin contact takes place when hands, sometimes hands and forearms, are immersed in chemical substances or a product. An example is shown in Figure 57 below. The good news is that the practice of immersing hands in chemicals isn't widespread now in the British manufacturing industry. However, workers such as hairdressers will be dependent on suitable gloves for immersion related activities such as hair dying, shampooing etc.

Figure 57[130] Immersion is one of the skin exposure pathways. In this case, it would be easy to use DIY "S" hooks to hold the pottery during coating and to drain the excess. The "s" hook will provide a SWD between the skin and the coating enamel. In many cases of immersion related skin exposure, simple approaches will help solve problems.

Direct contact with contaminated surfaces - Skin contact takes place when hands are intentionally used as a tool for handling or manipulating SHH containing or contaminated tools, equipment and workpieces. Examples can be seen in Figure 58.

Figure 58[130] The picture on the lefthand side shows a worker's hands and body in direct contact with contaminated equipment and the sun's UV rays. The picture on the righthand side shows a printing worker's hands in direct contact with solvents and

printing inks. The background shows that the work practices have the potential for creating splashes.

OSHKE

1. With reference to the pictures and activities seen in Figure 58, what could be done to avoid direct skin contact with SHH? *In the case of the construction worker, modern high visibility PPE will provide protection against UV exposure. The extent of work rate caused by holding a heavy ready mix concrete delivery hose and the associated skin contact can be managed by introducing an improved hydraulic delivery system (Figure 59 below) and a suitably designed handle to hold the delivery hose to direct pouring. In the case of printing works, components are manually cleaned using solvents. The activity could be undertaken in a specialised washing system suitable for the parts being cleaned, avoiding the need for direct contact-based cleaning shown in Figure 58. Suitable gloves could be worn for protection against minor contamination during products transfer - in and out of a washing system.*

Figure 59 Automated, extending hydraulic delivery systems, avoiding the need to manual-drag delivery hoses. A significantly improved work method when compared to the one shown in Figure 58.

Splashing - Splashes can land on the skin or clothing. This takes place when liquids, liquids-based mixes or powders are involved. Careless or inappropriate handling of liquids, liquid/solid mixes and dusty materials can cause significant splashing (Figure 60). Solvent splashes landing on clothing may produce a vapour cloud in the BZs of workers, leading to inhalation exposure. Solvents may be absorbed via the skin; or may cause damage to the surface of the skin. Similarly, dust splashing on clothing can cause inhalation exposure as well as damage to the skin, including sensitisation (Figure 60). In this case, sensitising dust penetrated the clothing and contacted the skin. Wearing PPE, including footwear, is not the end. It should be selected and used correctly and kept clean. Work practices led to surface contamination caused by splashing is self-evident in both pictures.

Figure 60[130] Splashes created by work activities can contaminate PPE and the Skin. SHH can cause dermatitis, both irritant and allergic types.

Deposition - This can happen when airborne contaminants impact or settle on the skin. Contaminants can be in the form of gas, vapour, dust, fibres, fume, or liquid mists. Figure 61 shows the after-effects of liquid-based aerosols in the air landing on the body.

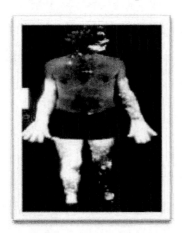

Figure 61[130] Liquid-based aerosols in air deposited on the skin. The extensive contamination seen in this Figure took place during brush application of a fence coating, which was dosed with a fluorescent tracer to help monitor skin contamination. The operator was working outdoors, wore a pair of shorts and a T-shirt. The pattern of contamination observed with the help of a fluorescent tracer makes the clothing arrangement obvious.

7.4 Applying safe working distance (SWD) for avoiding skin exposure

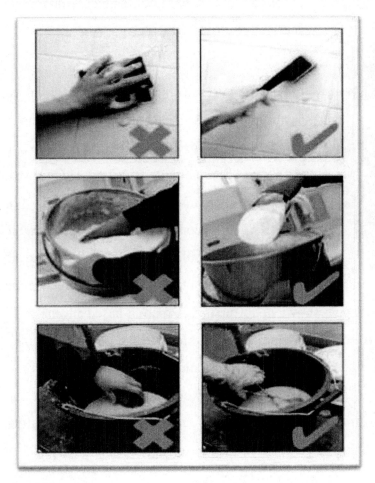

Figure 62[130] Distancing the skin from chemicals and wet-work. Example approaches are shown.

To comply with COSHH good control practice and the need to apply a SWD[22], efforts should be made to create adequate SWD between the hands and SHH. This HSE poster illustrates the SWD concept.

Skin exposure resulting from activities involving immersion should be controlled. At present, shampooing and colouring hair are examples where it is not reasonably practicable to avoid hand immersion. In situations like these, suitable gloves should be worn.

Direct contact with contaminated surfaces can be avoided by applying simple modifications to work activities. And in cases where it is not reasonably practical to avoid direct handling and justified in a RA, suitable gloves and other PPE should be worn.

Figure 63[130] The operator's gloved hand is in direct contact with contaminants due to an ineffective cleaning method.

This Figure shows a worker being involved in the process of disposing of unused printing ink. Although gloves were used, a suitable and sufficient RA should have concluded that practical alternatives should be used. For example, a silicone-based (or other suitable types) spatula could be used for removing the excess ink. This would create a suitable SWD to minimise skin contact and helped to reduce the amount of solvent needed for hand cleaning, as shown in the picture. A spatula-based cleaning will make the job easy, providing an effective cleaning approach (just think of cake making at home), and it is a green chemistry approach. Any remaining fine layers could be cleaned using a solvent-dipped wipe on a tool with a handle. The cuff of the glove is badly contaminated. It suggests that work practices may allow internal contamination of the glove as well as presenting difficulties with safe donning and removal of contaminated gloves. The prevention approach could have been implemented by making just-in-time amounts for minimising waste.

If SHH to health are **splashing** onto the skin, it would suggest that the work activities have serious exposure control shortcomings (Figures 60 and 63). In these cases, good control practices should be applied. If **deposition** on the skin from the air is an appreciable problem, it would suggest that the inhalation exposure isn't adequately controlled. In essence, approaches for controlling skin exposure to SHH should move away from gloves to technology-based handling.

7.5 Technology and skin exposure control

Dermal exposure risk management does not always have to involve high-tech solutions. Simple but effective technical approaches can also be applied to prevent or adequately control skin exposure. Examples of skin exposure control approaches are described below.

- **Eliminating** completely the use of hazardous substances: For example, eliminating the use of lead in paints and petrol; benzene as a common industrial solvent; and limiting the crystalline silica content in abrasive blasting sand. A prevention approach, in general, requires considerable technological innovation. Therefore, approaches based on prevention tend to develop through regulatory and commercial initiatives.

- **Changing the methods of work:** Epoxy resins are known to cause allergic contact dermatitis. However, these resins are an essential part of modern-day technology. Skin often comes into contact with these substances. It can happen when the two parts of the products are mixed (accelerator and base), as illustrated in Figure 60, and when the mixed resin is used in work activities. There are many practicable technical approaches for minimising skin exposure. Three examples are shown in Figure 64. The product container on the far left has a blue portion. It contains the required amount of the accelerator (no need for weighing). After removing the blue cap and manipulating the in-built system, the accelerator will come into contact with the base resin. Using the porthole created, a suitable paddle mixer could be used for thorough mixing. The approach prevents hands from coming into contact during weighing and manual pouring of the accelerator. The middle picture shows a system where the required amount of base and accelerator could be mixed as and when required using a specially designed plunger-based dispensing accessory. On the right, suitable approaches are shown for mixing the accelerator with the base resin. Construction industry has introduced many innovative approaches for minimising skin and inhalation exposure to sensitising/corrosive chemicals – can you think of a few?

Figure 64 Examples of approaches for mixing epoxy resin components.

- **Substituting hazardous substances with non-hazardous substance:** Solvents are used for removing crusted carbon, corrosion products and paints from jet engines. The use of dry carbon dioxide as an alternative is gaining momentum. The same technique may be applied in other areas of industrial activities where solvents are used for cleaning purposes.

- **Using a different form of the same substance for preventing exposure** – Enzyme based detergents are well-known respiratory and skin sensitisers. During product manufacture and use, airborne enzyme dust can settle on surfaces and clothing, causing secondary exposures. In order to deal with this problem, the industry reformulated the enzymes from fine powders into encapsulated granules or made them in liquid form. These modifications led to a significant reduction in sensitisation among production workers and users.

- **Using an alternative, less hazardous substance** - Skin sensitising, carcinogenic hexavalent chromium compounds have been widely used in dip coating and electrolytic plating metal articles. However, regulatory pressures have forced the industry to switch to less harmful trivalent chromium for many applications.

- **Using a different process** - Dichloromethane had been widely used in paint stripping. To reduce inhalation and skin exposure, alternative approaches have come into use, such as using n-butyl propionate.

- **Totally enclosing the process or the handling system** - These approaches can create opportunities for preventing or controlling inhalation and skin exposure. They are widely used in a variety of applications, such as volatile liquid filling stations, vapour recovery systems, and in paints mixing and filling.

- **Using suitable personal protective equipment** - Although the use of gloves and coveralls are commonplace in many workplaces. There are many situations where incorrectly selected gloves are used as the first line of protection. Although the situation is getting better, more can be done. If you are not an expert in the selection of adequate and suitable gloves, it is advisable to provide all the relevant information to a BSIF approved PPE supplier. They should have the knowledge to recommend the right product. Alternatively, you may use the HSE checklist[183] for consulting your glove supplier. There is a British Standard[99], based on the COSHH-CB approach, providing help for selecting chemical protective coveralls.

7.6 Summary

The extent of skin exposure to SHH has been coming down over the years. The technological advances (those in place and those emerging) are going to help deliver further significant reduction in skin exposure over time. There is a need for caution, using new technology for life improvements will not always lead to exposure reduction. So, vigilance is key for developing control measures before problems arise.

Chapter 8: Leading Indicators for Determining Exposure Control Effectiveness

"The secret of change is to focus all your energy, not on fighting the old, but on building the new."

- *Socrates. A Greek philosopher.*

8.1 Introduction

Personal exposure monitoring (inhalation, skin and biological) data is a type of leading indicator of exposure control status. It should help you investigate the nature and extent of employee exposure to SHH, as well as for assessing the effectiveness of control measures. An introduction to the subject can be found in HSE guidance, HSG173[184]. Those OSH practitioners wanting to develop a greater understanding of the subject can consult 'Monitoring for health hazards at work'[185].

Here is a caution, a (personal) exposure monitoring value on its own, for example, 0.5 mg/m3 TWA silica dust in the air, will not provide comprehensive information on exposure control effectiveness unless accompanied by associated core information[184], which includes relevant exposure modifiers observed during sampling. Furthermore, we learnt in Section 1.7 that an exposure value below WEL alone would not be enough for complying with the requirements of adequate exposure control.

OSHKE

1. Why do you think that a personal exposure monitoring value on its own will not provide comprehensive information on exposure/exposure control effectiveness? *For example, 0.1 mg/m3 TWA silica dust exposure value will not tell us, for example, whether: (i) dust was controlled at source and how; (ii) RPE was used. If used, was it correctly selected, including the right APF and filter, correctly, used and maintained; (iii) the activity complied with good practice requirements.*

This Chapter explores an alternative and describes COSHH generic leading indicators termed Exposure Control Indicators (ECIs) for checking the potential for exposure and exposure control effectiveness. These are based on the work of HSE[186,187,188], and fit within the context of business operational effectiveness assessment [49,189-197], such as:

- To maximise efficient use of resources in business operations.

- To ensure the organisation is achieving adequate RoI from their investment decisions.

- To improve quality, productivity and competitive positioning.

- To facilitate adapting to the ever-changing political, economic, social and technological environments.

- To foster knowledge, trust and respect among operational colleagues.

- To ensure that the organisation is operating within the requirements of COSHH.

- To target OSH resources on those activities giving rise to 'serious health effects' (Section 4.6) and for applying proportionate risk prevention/control measures.

8.2 A headline introduction to leading indicators

HSE and many other leading OSH organisations recognise the need for suitable and reliable leading exposure control effectiveness indicators. They consider that developing, collecting and using well-thought-out, robust, targeted, codified and benchmarked (BM) ECIs are no longer a new or novel concept[198-202.] As an example, the American Industrial Hygiene Association[198] proposed a definition for leading indicators as *"A measurable, meaningful, actionable, evidenced-based indicator that can be used to monitor, predict, influence or manage exposures, hazards actions and conditions of work that may impact worker health and well-being."*

8.3 Developing and using leading Exposure Control Indicators (ECIs) in COSHH-RM

This Chapter provides examples of COSHH related codified ECIs and their BMs. You are invited to:

- Consider their contribution to business RoI and control effectiveness checking/monitoring.

- Use them at your workplace.

- Influence your respective professional organisations to come together for developing nationally agreed ECIs for work-related health priority areas, along with their supporting ECI mobile apps.

- Promote wider use of ECIs in RM.

There is no single reliable leading indicator measure of COSHH-RM performance. This reflects the fact that RM typically requires a 'package' of measures in place to achieve adequate control[21]. Similarly, a 'package/basket of ECIs are needed on a range of key COSHH-RM measures[203]. This 'road-map' is no different to other areas of business activities (e.g. sales, marketing, production and ways of minimising taxation liabilities), requiring business intelligence for evidence-based decisions making. ECIs collected over a period should provide reliable trend indications on exposure control effectiveness. As you know, HSE's occupational ill-health statistics provide trend indications, but there are lagging indicators.

ECIs should be used judiciously to improve performance. They should not create unnecessary paperwork, resource pressures, cost and bureaucracy, but they should help identify:

(i) Areas of exposure control effectiveness.

(ii) Aspects of control failures leading and likely to cause excessive exposure (preferably supported by pictures for improving communication and reinforcing the ECI findings).

(iii) Areas complying/failing with the requirements of the COSHH 'principles of good practice'.

(iv) What urgent corrective actions are needed to rectify exposure control deficiencies.

8.4 About ECIs

In summary, ECIs should:

- **Measure the direct and indirect precursors to harm.** *Precursors are events, conditions (e.g. excessive exposure to SHH, failures in LEV design), circumstances or factors (e.g. no fourteen month LEV TExT, and inadequately maintained LEV) that precede a desired or undesired outcome (e.g. exposure to SHH and ill health), and to which it is linked through a control failure causal chain.*

- **Give advance warning before an event occurs that might lead to an undesired outcome(s).** These are known as **proxy, surrogate** or *indirect indicators.* A proxy *indicator is an indirect sign or measure that can approximate or can be representative of a phenomenon without the presence of a direct sign or measure, such as occupational asthma. In other words, proxy indicators are substitutes for gauging the likely exposure to SHH and the resulting health effect. They are more easily measured, captured and analysed than the true or lagging indicator (e.g. chronic ill health).*

- **Provide an early opportunity for preventive action to be taken.**

In other words, the chosen critical ECIs should be *proactive measures of the status of prevention/control efforts and can be observed and recorded prior to* undesired outcomes such as the likelihood of injuries, illness, or fatalities. Critical COSHH ECIs may include information on:

- At source control measures, including the substitution of less hazardous SHH and/or innovative controls,
- PPE,
- Attitudes/behaviours, and
- Organisational practices, such as undertaking RA and providing training, supervision and welfare facilities.

8.5 A summary of desirable usability characteristics of codified ECIs with BMs

This paragraph summarises examples of desirable characteristics of an ECI[198-200]:

- Integrated with the overall business objective and the context of RM system.
- Frameable with overall organisational performance measures, including OSH.
- Observable and/or measurable and actionable.
- Able to demonstrate cause and effect relationship.
- Able to provide robust early signals/information on control measures in place.
- Helps to demonstrate trends.
- Should not encourage unwanted or wasteful behaviours.
- Provide timely information.

- Safety representatives and operatives can use the information for seeking compliance and control.

- Should help create a positive organisational OSH culture.

8.6 A list of COSHH-ECIs

An example list of COSHH-generic ECIs are presented in appendix 8.1. Their supporting BM descriptions are in appendix 8.2. If you prefer task-based ECIs (e.g. working with metal working fluids, isocyanate mists, wood dust, silica dust and foundry fume/dust), you can develop your own set of task-based ECIs with the help of Appendix 8.1 and HSE's relevant COSHH Essentials direct advice sheets[92]. It is worth noting that if your risk assessment has determined that a few simple control measures are adequate, then working through a long list of generic or task-based ECIs may not be necessary, reflect this statement with RA for using household bleach, described in Chapter 4.

8.7 Summary

Leading indicators are 'at the moment or right-now' control effectiveness monitoring tools, whereas lagging indicators are long after the event tools. The time is right for OSH practitioners to use COSHH-ECIs, as like in safety, for example, safe working load indicators, height restriction indicators, alarmed guards and so on. For work-health RM, step changes in OSH culture are overdue. ECIs discussed in this Chapter provide opportunities.

Appendix 8.1

COSHH – generic Exposure Control Indicators (ECIs) for checking/monitoring control effectiveness		
Company Name: **Department and production area:** **Task:** **ECI checks carried out by, and date** **Task Location** (circle the one that applies): 1. Indoor; 2. Outdoor; 3. Confined Space **Task duration** (circle the one that applies)**:** 1. Performed routinely throughout the day. 2. As and when required during the day and takes less than an hour in total. 3. Infrequent task, undertaken as and when required. **SHH Details: What form** (circle all that apply): 1. Dust. 2. Fume. 3. Mist. 4. Vapour. 5. gas. **Health hazards:**		
To answer – Yes or No, read notes below this Table and Benchmarks (BM) in Appendix 8.2.	Yes	No
1. **Work in confined space (CS)** (If yes; answer next two ECI questions.)		
1.1. Safe working practices (including for emergencies) in operation as per the safe system of work in place.		
1.2. Operators know how to deal with CS emergencies and rehearsed.		
2. **Substitution considered** (requirement of COSHH.)		
2.1. If substitution is implemented, describe the approach. (See examples in BM Table.)		
3. **Containment, automation or other technical approaches implemented** (See examples in BM Table.)		
3.1. Describe the approaches implemented.		
4. **Local Exhaust Ventilation (LEV) provided.** (If yes; answer next seven ECIs)		
4.1. LEV system, including hoods, designed by competent person (CP) and certified suitable for task.		
4.2. LEV system (as designed) was installed and tested by CP and certified as working correctly.		
4.3. LEV system appears to function correctly.		
4.4. LEV hoods capture or receiving distance marked and operators place items within them.		
4.5. LEV users carry out routine checks and any defects corrected promptly.		
4.6. LEV 14 monthly maintenance by CP, passed TExT, and it is current.		
4.7. Recirculating LEV returned air quality tested regularly. (Skip, this ECI, if no recirculating LEV.)		
5. **USE Mechanised General Ventilation (MGV) for exposure control** (If yes; answer next two ECIs)		

5.1. MGV system designed and installed by CP and certified suitable for task.		
5.2. MGV maintained by CP.		
6. Respiratory Protective Equipment (The term RPE – includes respirators and BA) **provided.** (If yes; answer next four ECIs)		
6.1. If respirators provided, they are adequate and suitable and used correctly.		
6.2. If BA provided, they are adequate and suitable and used correctly.		
6.3. All RPE types: when not in use, stored in a clean environment.		
6.4. All reusable RPE types: maintained in accordance with manufacturers' instructions.		
7. Skin Protection Measures (If yes; answer next two ECI questions.)		
7.1. Skin exposure control measures adequate and suitable.		
7.2. Gloves and other PPE suitable, used correctly (including donning/doffing), and when not in use stored correctly.		
8. Facilities for washing, changing, eating and drinking.		
8.1. They are adequate, suitable, kept clean and maintained.		
9. Organisation and Management.		
9.1. COSHH RA adequate and suitable, kept up to date and records kept if more than five employees.		
9.2. Operatives consulted on matters of COSHH RM including control measures.		
9.3. Suitable information, instruction and training provided to operatives and supervisors.		
9.4. Active supervision in place to ensure operatives use control measures correctly.		
9.5. Health surveillance provided, where it is appropriate for protecting operatives' health and no warnings raised.		
9.6. Personal exposure monitoring carried out, where justified in RA, indicates exposures below tolerable levels.		

Notes to help complete the observations on COSHH-Generic ECIs.

(i) Using ECIs is not a legal requirement. Designing, installing, checking, testing and maintaining control measures are required by law.

(ii) ECIs focus on: the provision of correct design, installation, use, checking and maintenance of control measures; and the standards of welfare facilities, organisation and management.

(iii)'Yes' or 'No' answer to an ECI should be based on BM and what have seen and shown (e.g. fourteen monthly LEV TExT report) and discussion with operatives and supervisors during a limited observation of the task. This is known as a walkthrough assessment.

(iv)BMs should help you identify areas of exposure control strengths and areas requiring actions to ensure adequate control of exposure. It should help in gaining an understanding of how well the COSHH-RM efforts are supporting operational effectiveness.

(v) For an ECI to achieve a 'Yes' answer, all elements of the ECI descriptors should be in place for all operatives/task stations observed. Relevant BM will support a decision.

(vi)COSHH-ECIs do not cover safety issues (e.g. fire) and other health related issues such as hearing, well-being and manual handling.

(vii)   A person who is familiar with the task being assessed, SHH in use, the control requirements, the relevant ECIs in this Table, and their associated BMs should be able to complete the assessment quickly. (It is like learning to drive a car and then driving it routinely). Decide whether this investment is proportional and prudent for RM purposes.

(viii)   Make sure the occupier/employer, supervisors, managers and operatives are aware and understand the above points and the inter-relationships between ECIs, COSHH and operational management.

Appendix 8.2

COSHH-Generic ECIs and their Benchmarking (BM) descriptors
TASK involving the SHH, where does it take place?
Indoor: Work is taking place inside a building or a covered space/area. Examples: A workshop, a room, a garage with open doors, a compartment in a ship or a covered outdoor area such as a tent, trailer box etc. Note: Some of the example areas could rapidly become CS due to work activities. For example, a garage with an open door when spray painting a car or welding or engine left running.
Outdoor: Work is taking place in an open-air space or in an area not under cover or shelter. Free unimpeded air movement. Examples: Welding on a railway line, spray painting the outer-hull of a boat/ship. Activity is taking place not in any fixed or temporary covering, etc.
Confined space (CS): The space is substantially enclosed or largely enclosed, and which also has the specified risk to workers (any one of these or combined): of fire; explosion; loss of consciousness caused by noxious fumes, gases and vapours; asphyxiation due to lack of oxygen; or drowning, due to sudden release of SHH, water, grain etc.; or it is reasonably foreseeable that any of these risks may arise during a work activity. Read CS Regulations. Examples: A small workshop, a room, a garage with open doors, storage tanks, sewers, bilges, silos, reaction vessels, drains, a compartment in a ship or a covered outdoor area such as a tent, trailer box etc.
Task Duration
Performed routinely throughout the day: Task performed every day and occupies one or more hours of the working day. May be repeated several times.
As and when required during the day and takes less than an hour in total: Undertaken when demand arises (e.g. flame cutting a corroded exhaust mount on a car). Odd jobs put together take less than an hour of the working day, even if repeated more than once.
Infrequent, as and when required: These are tasks done as one-off when the demand is created, eg, emptying and replacing LEV dust collection bag.
1. Work in confined space
1.1. Safe working practices (including for emergencies) in operation as per the safe system of work in place: Discussion, documentation and observation indicate that so far as is reasonably practicable, if the entry cannot be prevented, (i) b*efore starting the work, the duty holder, where necessary supported by one or more CP, has developed a suitable safe system of work; (ii) it complies with CS regulations; (iii) Those affected by the CS work are aware of the system and understand its requirements; (iv)* when asked, if any shortcomings identified the responsible person and operatives can provide answers on how they would be rectified immediately; (v) operatives trained on safe working and discussion on the site supports it; (vi) supervision in place to ensure effective operation of the system. Note: Do your determination without entering the CS. **No suitable and adequate safe working practices in operation, work must stop immediately.**

142

1.2. Operators know how to deal with CS emergencies: (i) those work in CS know how to raise alarm for help; (ii) documentation and discussion show that the arrangements are regularly rehearsed to demonstrate readiness. **Note: Do your determination without entering the CS.**

2. Substitution considered (look out for those used widely in the task relevant industrial sector)

2.1. If substitution implemented, describe: Examples are described to help you decide and look out for others, where necessary:

1. Low boiling point isocyanates used in two pack paints; 2. Low fume welding electrodes used; 3. Water based cutting fluids instead of oil based; 4. Dust suppression technology used when using enzymes; 5. Water suppression during stone cutting instead of dry cutting; 6. Chrome three used in electroplating, instead of chrome six; 7. Chrome free or low chrome cement; 8. Latex free gloves used; 9. Powder free latex gloves used, where use cannot be prevented; 10. Dichloromethane not used for paint stripping, alternatives used; 11. Rosin free flux in soldering. 12. Use dishwashers, instead of hand washing in catering sectors.

3. Containment, automation or other technical approaches implemented.

3.1. If yes, describe the approach(es): Examples are described to help you decide and look out for others, where necessary. 1. Vacuum drying of wet components; 2. Plastic balls on the surface of electro plating liquids in a tank to control evaporation and mist; 3. Safe working distance created by things like S-hook, helping to prevent hand immersion; 4. Using a spatula to clean residues or excess products left in a mixing bucket; 5. Automated solvent dispensing instead of using manual methods; 6. Automated dough handling to avoid direct contact with skin; 7. Self-contained mixing of accelerators and base; 8. Barriers or alarms to prevent operators putting their BZ in the contaminated air zone; 9. Solvent cleaning of components using a suitable machine, instead of hand cleaning; 10. Using a mist splash prevention guards in front of cutting tool when using metal working fluid; 11. Enclosed spray booths: clearance time observed before lifting visor on RPE; 12. Arrangements in place to prevent operators' heads being placed in the path of contaminated air travelling into hoods; 13. Operator position marked to prevent them standing in the wrong places in front of LEV hoods; 14. Turn tables provided to make the job easy for an operator and helping to reduce exposure; 15. Anti-froth system used for minimising mist dispersion in cooling towers; 16. Dip-slide tests for ensuring the quality of the product, such as metalworking fluids in sumps; 17. Users of LEV hoods know the capture/receiving distances of their hoods; 18. Cameras in place to help improve control practice; 19. Clear signs indicating what should be done, for example, respirator zone and booths' contaminant clearance times must be observed; 20. High efficiency spray guns are used for minimising mist and product wastage.

4. Local Exhaust Ventilation (LEV) provided.

4.1. LEV system, including hoods, designed by competent person (CP) and certified suitable for task: self-explanatory.

4.2. LEV system (as designed) installed and tested by CP and certified as working correctly: self-explanatory.

4.3. LEV system appears to function correctly: (Look out for examples) 1. Where installed, air flow indicators on hoods show hoods are working correctly; 2. Areas around the hoods have no fine dust layers; 3. No fine dust layer on the outside surfaces of hoods; 4. Hoods are not damaged; 5. No obvious leaks through hoods and ducting; 6. Where flow diverters in place, their housing and baffles are not damaged; 7. Capture distance marked on hoods; 8. No DIY repairs to hoods and ducting; 9. No dust layers or heap of dust in the areas surrounding dust collector bags and their housing; 9. Work surfaces kept clean and free of contaminants; 10. Compressed air NOT used for clearing dust on surfaces including tools and PPE - In these situations, cleaned with industrial grade vac cleaner, with high efficiency filter; 11. Using broom for sweeping up SHH is highly restricted, encourage correct use of LEV; 12. Where smoke tube/anemometer could be used, smoke/air flow indicates good extraction within the capture bubble.

4.4. LEV hoods capture or receiving distance marked and operators place items within them. There are several ways to mark. Operators are trained to place items within the zones and active supervision is place to ensure good working practice.

4.5. LEV users carry out routine checks and any defects corrected promptly: 1. Users check hoods air flow indicators to make sure they are operating within range; 2. Users check/lookout for damage to hoods, ducting and flow diverters; 3. No dust leakage outside hoods or through ducting; 4. Any visible seals on systems are in good order. Discuss with some users to understand practice.

4.6. LEV 14 monthly maintenance by CP, passed TExT, and it is current: Self-explanatory.

4.7. Recirculating LEV returned air quality tested regularly: This test is needed to ensure recirculated air is of acceptable quality. Ask how do they do it. Tests can be done in a number of ways, including flow resistance, contaminant level monitoring, and pressure drop monitoring. Filter housing appear sound and no signs of contaminant leak. Filters changed as recommended by the manufacturer/designer/date and marked.

5. Use Mechanised General Ventilation (MGV) for exposure control

5.1. MGV system designed by CP and certified suitable for task: Self-explanatory.

5.2. MGV maintained by CP: Documentation available to confirm.

6. Respiratory Protective Equipment (RPE - respirators and/or Breathing Apparatus (BA)) **provided.**

6.1. If respirators provided, it is adequate and suitable and used correctly: 1. Right for the task, job, wearer and the working environment;

2. Right filter including assigned protection factor, fitted correctly and in-date; 3. Used correctly - fit testing undertaken, where necessary, worn correctly, recommended pre-use checks carried out. Discuss with a sample of users.

6.2. If BA provided, they are adequate and suitable and used correctly: 1. Right for the task, job, wearer and the working environment;

2. Right assigned protection factor; 3. Breathing quality air supplied; 4. Used correctly – fit testing undertaken, where necessary, worn correctly, recommended pre-use checks carried out. Discuss with a sample of users.

6.3. All RPE types: when not in use, stored in a clean environment: Self-explanatory. Discuss with a sample of users.

6.4. All RPE types: maintained in accordance with manufacturers' instructions: Seek evidence – records, RA, discuss with a sample of users.

7. Skin Protection Measures

7.1. Skin exposure control measures adequate and suitable: Which skin exposure pathways are evident. Measures in place - should adequately control the skin exposure. Find out how was the decision made to arrive at adequacy and suitability.

7.2. Gloves and other PPE suitable, used correctly (including donning/doffing), and when not in use stored correctly: 1. Ask supervisors, how do they establish the suitability of gloves and PPE used – with the help of a CP, HSE guidance, supplier, product label/safety data sheet; 2. Ask a sample of users for donning/doffing demonstration; 3. observe storage methods.

8. Facilities for washing, changing, eating and drinking.

8.1. They are adequate, suitable, kept clean and maintained: 1. Adequate toilets and hand basins – check against recommendations in INDG293; 2. Clean and maintained facilities - are they in a state that you would not hesitate to use them; 3. Hot and cold running water available with cleansing/skin care agents or suitable alternatives provided (wet-wipes, urns etc.); 4. Rest area has tables and chairs, kept clean and tidy.

9. Organisation and Management.

9.1. COSHH RA adequate and suitable, kept up to date and records kept if more than five employees: 1. Check against HSE recommendations; 2. Kept up to date - review dates in place and actions taking place as marked in RA and when complete signed off;

3. Records kept, if more than five employees. Accuracy, suitability and precision of RA is priority and not the paper mountain.

9.2. Operatives consulted on matters of COSHH RM including control measures: Evidence to this ECI could be found during discussion with a sample of operatives.

9.3. Suitable information, instruction and training provided to operatives and supervisors: 1. Discussion with operatives and supervisors, checked against RA and work practices observed would indicate; 2. Operatives aware of hazards, risks and health outcomes from excessive exposure to the SHH; 3. Know and understand the control measures needed and how to use them correctly.

9.4. Active supervision in place to ensure operatives use control measures correctly: 1. Observe the task and the way it is carried out; 2. Discussion with operatives and supervisors and checks against RA and work practices observed would indicate; 3. Signs of inadequate supervision include - safe and healthy working is not a priority; getting the job done comes first; unsafe work practices overlooked; Cleanliness and tidy workshop isn't a priority. Supervisors unaware of hazards, risks, RAs, controls required and don't appear to take responsibility.

9.5. Health surveillance (HS) provided, where it is appropriate for protecting operatives' health and no warnings raised: 1. RA provide justification as to why HS is needed. Many employers mistakenly opt to HS as a soft option to providing adequate exposure control and complying with good practice. No adverse observation raised, by the CP, following HS.

9.6. Personal exposure monitoring carried out, where justified in RA, indicates exposures below tolerable levels: 1. Is the requirement justified in RA. 2. Just complying with the limited number of WELs will not satisfy the adequate control requirements. 3. ECI findings may be supported by measurements.

Notes:

For BM familiarisation purposes, refer to inadequate exposure control issues described/discussed in Tables and OSHKE, and those shown in Figures in this book.

Chapter 9: Efficient and Effective Decision Making

"Basically, to lead without a title is to derive your power within the organisation not from your position but from your competence, effectiveness, relationships, excellence, innovation and ethics."

- *Robin. S. Sharma, Canadian Lawyer.*

9.1 Introduction

So far, we have explored the technical aspects of COSHH-RM. From now on, we will explore some of the supporting managerial matters. Although some of these issues are highlighted in previous Chapters, from now on, they will be explored a bit more to support you. This Chapter briefly explores efficient and effective decision making.

9.2 Efficiency and effectiveness

Late Peter Drucker, a management guru, described **efficiency** as **"doing things right"**, and **effectiveness** as **"get the right things done"**[205]. As an example, an OSH practitioner completing or getting others to complete 99% of COSHH RAs and getting them recorded in a highly sophisticated COSHH database within the agreed time could be considered as efficiency (output). Doing adequate and suitable RAs, recording them in HSE RA template and using these assessments to deliver the required results, (for those at risk), which are proportionate, timely and cost-prudent, is effective. It means achieving 'adequate control of exposure to comply with law' and a good RoI (outcomes).

To explore and explain his thoughts on efficiency and effectiveness, Drucker interviewed many executives and experts. The information he gathered led him to say that things such as intelligence, imagination, knowledge, creativity, skills, experience and training are essential resources. They set limits to what can be achieved, but only effectiveness converts them into desired results, reinforced by several essential 'practices' summarised in Table 15 below. Using Drucker's thesis, I have borrowed one of his metaphors to summarise the contents of his book[205]: "common people achieving uncommon achievement." It is a good metaphor for OSH practitioners because you rely on the knowledge created by many specialists, strategists and policy makers.

Table 15 Essential practices for delivering effectiveness.

Essential practices	Explanation
Rigorously recording where the time goes.	This practice should prod and nudge for greater effectiveness. Help reduce time-wasters (activities). Improve the level and quality of outcomes.
Focussing vision on contribution.	This element should shift efforts from procedures to conceptions (ideas/innovation). Mechanics to analysis (RA example explanation above). Outputs to outcomes.
Making strengths productive.	Putting value systems into action. Respecting the person's capacity, capabilities, inventiveness and achievements, and creating opportunities for the person as well as the organisation to achieve the organisation's goals.
First thing first.	Leadership of dedication, determination and endurance for achieving the organisation's goals - Make it happen. For example, dealing first with serious health hazards/effects instead of minor health hazards/effects; a short, effective RA delivering effective control, instead of concentrating on lengthy RAs and filing them.
Effective decisions.	Its essence is an ethics of action and right decisions in sequence. Applying COSHH good control practice.

9.3 At the "coalface"

The availability of a mountain of national and international OSH Standards, HSE's COSHH related exposure control guidance and research reports, along with a vast array of specialism related reports have become highly noticeable. Examples of specialisms include, biological sciences, chemical sciences, engineering design and technology, ergonomics or human factors, health-statistics, industrial toxicology, socio-economics, occupational hygiene, occupational medicine, occupational nursing, physical sciences, process control technology, sociology and work psychology.

For OSH practitioners to support effective COSHH compliance at the 'coalface', it is necessary to get to know and understand the basics of specialist knowledge, interpret it and apply that knowledge to workplace exposure control needs. In addition, there is an increasing demand and expectation to acquire and apply management, finance, computing and communication skills. Also, as noted in chapters 3 and 4, there is a demand for simplification of expert and specialist knowledge, making them usable at the coalface. To that end, this book is making a contribution.

So, let us mirror the availability of extensive OSH knowledge and support resources with medicine. Despite the rapid advances in knowledge, technology and medical diagnostics, there is a requirement for a medical doctor to elicit an accurate clinical history before proceeding to use medical diagnostics and treating the patient. Likewise, despite the vast expansion of OSH specialist knowledge, engineering and technological sophistications, OSH practitioners must effectively interact and communicate with operatives, supervisors, managers and other OSH CPs to understand practical exposure control needs and help devise and implement adequate and suitable exposure control measures. This is where Drucker's essential practices become relevant to every OSH practitioner.

9.4 Competence and prudence

OSH practitioners at all levels are likely to be subject to increased litigation and scrutiny[44,46,53,54,55,56,206]. And, there is a constant worry among OHS practitioners about what might become of ambulance/insurance chasers. These factors may unintentionally influence the mode of operation of many OSH practitioners. So, competency in decision making and its delivery must be evident and should withstand scrutiny. It means that **an employer must ensure that any individual performing a task on their behalf has the right competence** to do a task, without putting their OSH practitioners and others at 'significant risk'[206,207]. HSE's description of OSH competence is: the combination of training, skills, experience and knowledge that a person has and their ability to perform a task safely[208]. Other factors such as attitudes and physical ability can affect someone's competence[208]. For example, the factors identified in official reports[44,52-55], such as creating excessive paper work, "empire building", self-rule making, and insisting on going beyond the requirements of the law. OSH professional bodies and OSHCR have a big role to play to ensure that another report by HSE or a government would not come to conclusions like those expressed in references such as 44,46,52-55.

9.5 A suggestion for assessing the effectiveness of OSH delivery

The summary relationship between proportionality and effectiveness in OSH-RM is summarised in Figure 65 below. Schedule 2A of COSHH sets out eight principles of "good control" practice (Chapter 1). Grounded on the discussions so far and Figure 65, OSH professionals may wish to create a simple, open and accountable eight principles of OSH good practice.

- I know and understand my competency envelope (boundary) and practice within it.
- I maintain the highest standards of professional endeavour, integrity, confidentiality and personal conduct.
- I take account of the key human and system factors in play and apply them as appropriate to help deliver compliance.
- I apply the 'so far as is reasonably practicable' requirement, proportionality and prudence when recommending or implementing RM measures.
- I use effective tools and techniques for delivering training and communicating RM related information.
- I avoid 'rules community blue-tape' and 'gold-plating' burdens when initiating, helping or supporting effective compliance.
- I display personal service quality labels to inform my practice standards (a potential example in Figure 65).
- I maintain self-development (Continuous Professional Development) to keep pace with OSH related developments that will inform, shape and maintain my competency envelope.

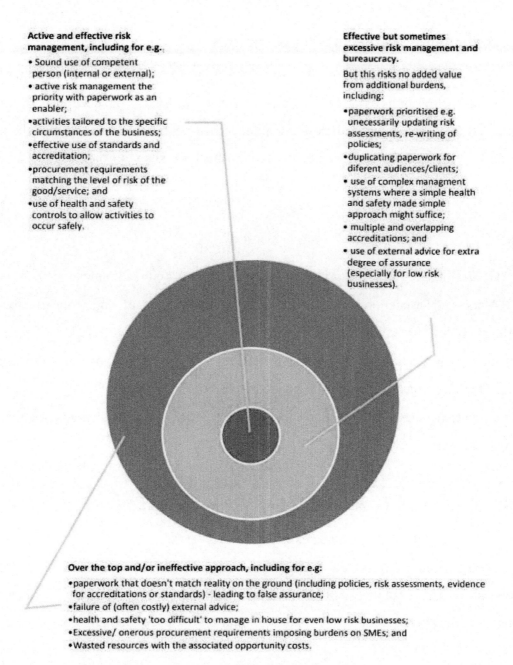

Active and effective risk management, including for e.g.

• Sound use of competent person (internal or external);
• active risk management the priority with paperwork as an enabler;
• activities tailored to the specific circumstances of the business;
• effective use of standards and accreditation;
• procurement requirements matching the level of risk of the good/service; and
• use of health and safety controls to allow activities to occur safely.

Effective but sometimes excessive risk management and bureaucracy.

But this risks no added value from additional burdens, including:

• paperwork prioritised e.g. unecessarily updating risk assessments, re-writing of policies;
• duplicating paperwork for diferent audiences/clients;
• use of complex managment systems where a simple health and safety made simple approach might suffice;
• multiple and overlapping accreditations; and
• use of external advice for extra degree of assurance (especially for low risk businesses).

Over the top and/or ineffective approach, including for e.g:

• paperwork that doesn't match reality on the ground (including policies, risk assessments, evidence for accreditations or standards) - leading to false assurance;
• failure of (often costly) external advice;
• health and safety 'too difficult' to manage in house for even low risk businesses;
• Excessive/ onerous procurement requirements imposing burdens on SMEs; and
• Wasted resources with the associated opportunity costs.

Figure 65[54]. An illustrated relationship between effective OSH management and blue tape.

For many OSH practitioners, an initiative of the kind described in this section is likely to provide a competitive edge against those practitioners targeted by several influential reports (9.4 above) and enforcement agencies. **The British OSH system** and the OSHCR[58] registrants **will benefit tremendously from those acting as change agents**, initiators/innovators, calculated risk takers, catalysts, unifying forces and success makers for compliance delivery and to meet head-on the kinds of concerns expressed regarding a small number of practitioners.

9.6 Anticipating inspectors' expectations

This section is not a comprehensive list of the subject matter, nor is it intended to read the minds of inspectors or provide a detailed description of HSE's inspection and enforcement policies. My personal thoughts below are intended to be helpful to your thought process to anticipate and engage with an inspector when an inspector visits your organisation for a 'general inspection'. **Formal inspections** can take different forms, and examples of inspections are listed below.

- General inspection of a workplace, most of the time, an unannounced visit.
- A focused inspection, in the main, deals with an issue of high concern, for example, activities involving crystalline silica.
- Incident inspection, after an accident causing a fatality, injury, or near miss, which could have resulted in an injury, or case of ill health and has been reported
- An intelligence-led inspection, for example, after complaints made relating to OHS situations at a place of work.

HSE and Local Authorities **target sectors, workplaces and activities**:

- Which have the most serious risks.
- Where they have information and intelligence that OSH is a significant concern, such as, previous performance, out breaks of OSH related situations, concerns raised by workers, the public or others, incident investigations and reports of injuries, diseases and dangerous occurrences.

The **publicised**[50,84] **approaches to HSE/LA inspection** include:

- Speak to relevant people, for example, managers, supervisors, workers, the OSH team and employee representatives.
- Observe a sample of workplace activities, conditions and practices.
- Assess relevant documents, if necessary.
- Check whether risk controls are effective.
- Identify any breaches of the law.

- Consider appropriate enforcement if found to be necessary.

On the matter of SHH and COSHH, there is no definitive guide because an inspection can highlight the unexpected. Basically, the list below is an example to help OSH practitioners to be prepared.

- Your organisation appears to be or is seen (using the five senses) as a "Kaizen". Briefly, it is a concept that refers to business activities that seek to continuously improve all functions.

- OSH policy is up to date, takes account of SHH/COSHH, and is actively implemented.

- Consult workforce on matters of OSH and take account and utilise information in RA/RM.

- COSHH RAs reflect common sense and proportionality. They are kept up to date and actively used.

- COSHH-RM is actively targeting those activities which have the potential for the most serious health risks.

- Visual inspection/observations can provide confidence that controls are effective. Leading ECIs (Chapter 8) should help you prepare.

- You are confident that the principles of good practice and the requirements for adequate exposure control is satisfied, especially for those COSHH activities giving rise to the potential for the most serious health risks.

- Competency can be felt/made evident and seen to be applied to COSHH-RM.

- Most relevant documentations/evidence is in place and actively managed. For example, RAs, LEV design, installation, use and maintenance, RPE selection, use and maintenance.

- Key compliance areas discussed in EMM[50,84] are managed to your satisfaction, and you are confident about the management.

- Work areas involved in SHH are kept clean as they can be. A dirty "COSHH" area can raise concerns.

- Welfare facilities are clean and tidy.

9.7 Summary

Based on the analysis so far, potential reflective messages could be summarised as follows. OSH practitioners, helping to deliver effective COSHH compliance, should:

- Initiate, develop and implement compliance-centred approaches for compliance with the law.

- Use simple, user-friendly, transparent, proportionate and accountable ways of assessing, implementing, reviewing and communicating adequate control of exposure to SHH.

- Focus on creating an environment for minimising "blue-tape" related 'rules', resources and expenditures.

- Include an appropriate quality ranking for OSH reports, advice, recommendations etc. (Figure 65).

- Consider developing eight OSH good practice principles to mirror COSHH "good control practice".

Chapter 10: Inspiring OSH Buy-In By Operational Management

"Positive changes can be tough at the start; can create enemies during the process; but are worth it at the end."

10.1 Introduction

There are legal, moral, social, and financial reasons for effective and efficient OSH-RM. OSH practitioners understand this model. But when it comes to selling OSH to operations, it appears that many of us would focus on legal, moral, and social motivators. It seems that, for many of us, taking account and including finance related arguments doesn't come as part of our territory. For that reason, many of us tend to ignore or park-aside the most important organisational motivator - money. It is rare to see in OSH reports about detailed accounting arguments such as how profitability and cost minimisation would be achieved by implementing an OSH solution.

Whenever we choose to include finance in OSH, most of us tend to use HSE published global sums[119] and snippets from HSE press releases, guidance documents and research reports. This book is not an exception. Unfortunately, global statistics may not gain sufficient attraction, close attention, and scrutiny of the operational teams because global information may not have easily discernible direct connections to their operational budgets, productivity, and delivery. This shouldn't come as a surprise, naturally, they are focussed on productivity, cashflow management, and profitability, whereas OSH is the anchor (or part of the solid mass) for all these. So, let us ask, where is the coupling that holds the anchor and the chain (operation)? This should be a basic question among OSH practitioners.

Therefore, **it is sensible that every OSH practitioner needs to learn and use the most common language - finance - of any business to maximise OSH buy-in.** It would make it easier to sell our 'products' (projects, training, exposure control solutions, etc.), ourselves, and our profession. It means blending-in all four drivers - legal, social, moral, and financial - in compelling, compassionate, and compliance centred ways. And this should happen every time OSH is being put on the table – as you know, a Court sentencing on OSH related matters takes finance into account.

10.2 Becoming an OSH salesperson

It is considered that every OHS practitioner needs to aspire to a new continuous professional development (CPD), 'inspiring OSH buy-in, which includes the **AIDA** concept'[209].

- **Awareness** - customers' awareness about your OSH 'product',
- **Interest** - customers becoming interested in your 'product',
- **Desire** - customers saying, I like the 'product,' and I want the 'product', and
- **Action** - customers buy the 'product'.

When attempting to create OSH-AIDA:

- Be knowledgeable (part of competency) about your OSH 'product',
- Make your 'product' attractive on all four drivers (legal, social, moral, and financial),
- Be inspiring to create the desire for your 'product', and
- Be ready to deliver your 'product' on time, with RoI factors and other relevant information built-in.

10.3 What does it entail?

Here are some thoughts:

- Engage with a business mind, where OSH is blended-in, not as a standalone, because it is a law and is morally and socially right.
- Time is money. It includes OSH related efforts and activities. Does it mean 'Safety First' is a cliché? You decide. Anyway, the cliché does not include health. Also reflect with reports such as lofstedt[44], Young[53] and Blue-tape[54,55]. Always remember, British law is about 'so far as is reasonably practicable'. This means risks vs. time, trouble, money, other resources, proportionality, prudence, and objectivity.
- Learn to look through the business microscope, where you should find, among other things, OSH on the slide.
- Walk and talk to deliver the OSH-AIDA.
- Build networks because relationships matter to inspire OSH buy-in.
- Keep your networks warm, buzzing, and welcoming. It means considerate and compassionate 'nursing'.

- Understand perceptions among your networks and manage perceptions with a business mindset and win over any negative perceptions.

- Win hearts and mind to achieve OSH buy-in.

- Reports are important aids to your OSH goals. They should be brief and address the strengths, weaknesses, opportunities, and threats associated with your 'product'. Don't just rely on the legal requirements as the strength, make sure it talks about exposure control RM and productivity strengths.

- Keep only the essential records. Always look for opportunities for minimising paper work, blue-tape[54-56] and gold plating[53]. Creating any unessential information costs time and money and keeps you away from your networks and 'walking and talking' the OSH-AIDA.

- Use effective risk communication principles and the nudging approach (Chapter 11).

- Understand essential financial terms and use them in your 'product' selling strategies.

- Take account of environmental and climate change implications.

It is conceivable that applying these footprints could help you to build a reputation and respect. They, in turn, should create confidence and "I can do it optimism." In essence, they create openings to get your OSH-AIDA buy-in. In this context, the book by Brian Tracy[210] on 'The Psychology of Selling' is an essential read for every aspiring OHS practitioner.

10.4 Building finance into OSH

Here are some ideas for your reflection.

- Become familiar with some of the key finance terms (Table 16) and their application.

- Make friends with accountants, financial controllers, buyers, product, contract and logistics managers to help build finance into OSH.

- Start practicing the art of blending finance into your OSH activities. Get it reviewed by your friendly networks.

- Be part of the solution to build cultures which help operations managers to work with their finance, legal, communication and OSH, and other risk management colleagues to get the input of other professionals and to deliver OSH 'products' to the right quality and to an agreed budget and time.

- Start applying the four motivators in your OSH-AIDA. But you cannot argue cost as a standalone factor for not complying with statutory duties.

According to HSE, **"something is reasonably practicable unless its costs are grossly disproportionate to the benefits."** For more information on this, see Risk management: Expert guidance - HSE principles for Cost Benefit Analysis in support of ALARP; and Risk management: Expert guidance - Cost Benefit Analysis (CBA) checklist (hse.gov.uk).

Some of you may argue I was hired to advise/manage and/or deliver OSH-RM measures. Just reflect this sentiment, for example, with that of a product, logistics or facilities manager. Very quickly, you will appreciate the importance of finance in your work, which should help you to create a desire for practising OSH-AIDA.

10.5 Examples of financial terms

Some of the key terms and their meanings are provided in Table 16.

Table 16 A brief descriptions of common finance terms relevant for the OSH-AIDA

Financial terms	About finance terms
Average order value	It is calculated by dividing the revenue amount for a period by the total number of orders placed in the period.
Backlog	It has several uses, including sales or service orders waiting to be delivered. For example, a stack of LEV TExt certificates related actions needing completion by OSH Cost Centre.
Booking (sales order)	Actioned (won, signed, or committed) sale where the purchase order has been received and approved.
Capital cost	Fixed, one-time expenses incurred on the purchase of items and/or materials used in the production of goods or services. Capital items are those that have an expected life of more than one year. They are recorded as fixed assets and are required to be depreciated each year. For example, investment in LEV system for manufacturing marble, granite, and hardwood fire surrounds by the production department.
Cash flow	It is a measure of the cash coming into the organisation and the cash going out of the business. It means that the amount of all monies (includes cash, cheques, and direct bank deposits) from sales and/or provision of service less all payments (includes cash, cheques, and direct bank payments) made by the business. In accounting terms, there is a distinct type of cash flow. **Operating cash flows** - those relating to the sales of goods and services; **Investment cash flows** - those relating to the purchase and disposal of fixed assets and long-term investments; and **Financing cash flows** – those relating to remaining cash through loans or share issues.

Financial terms	About finance terms
Cost centre	A separate department/unit within a business to which costs can be allocated and collected. This also includes departments/units that do not produce directly but incur costs to the business.
Net sales	The total amount of sales (products and/or services) made, within a specified time period by a business after deductions for discounts, returns and any taxes such as VAT included in the selling period.
Direct costs or Cost of goods /services sold	Known as COGS. All the costs incurred directly in producing a product or delivering a service (e.g. labour, materials, delivery etc.).
Gross profit	The profit of a business made after deducting the direct costs associated with the production and delivery of merchandise and/or services of the business. It is calculated as sales revenues less cost of goods sold (before deducting selling and administrative expenses). It means you need to deliver OSH prudently and efficiently to minimise OSH related expenses.
Operating expenses	Operating expenses (also referred to as general and administrative expenses) are the costs that are required to keep the business going day to day (e.g. rent, rates, utilities, marketing, etc.).
Net earnings, net profit, or bottom line	Earnings income after paying all expenditures, including production, administration, and any other sundry costs. Money 'to play' without incurring debts. It is calculated as operating profit less all expenses, including interest and taxation, before dividends.
Net Present Value (NPV)	NPV is the sum of future cash inflows and outflows of a long-term project from t_0 to t_n (where t_0 is the start year of the project and t_n is the end year of the project), discounted to the present (t_0) using an appropriate discount rate, usually the firm's weighted average cost of capital.

Financial terms	About finance terms
Operating profit or EBIT – Earnings before interest and taxes	Gross profit (as above) less operating expenses and before deduction of interest and taxes.

10.6 A hypothetical example on OSH perspective and OSH buy-in

A company manufactures high-quality granite and marble-based products. They contain crystalline silica. Excessive exposure to silica dust can cause serious lung diseases, including cancer.

The production work involves cutting and polishing with hand-held rotary tools. About three years ago, the company installed a LEV system on the recommendation of an OSH consultant, and the system was manufactured and installed by a firm specialising in high street shops ventilation. The system is based on three open-faced receiving hoods. A typical example is shown in Figure 66. The extraction hood and the LEV system did not prevent dust contaminated air (energised and released when using powered tools, see Figures 26 and 35), from entering the operatives' BZs and the surrounding areas. The potential for silica dust exposure is significant.

Figure 66 An example of an open-faced receiving hood.

Following a recent HSE inspection, the business was issued with two Improvement Notices (INs). One required that the dust extraction system should be thoroughly examined and tested as required by Regulations 9 of COSHH and the other required that the LEV should effectively capture dust generated from work activities and be removed from the BZ of operatives. It also required that adequate and suitable RPE with a minimum APF of 20 should be used for the dust creating tasks.

161

Due to a significant down turn in economic conditions, the business gained lower than expected bookings and consequently a low average order value and the cash flow is very tight. The backlog (orders waiting to be delivered) was significant and extended over a period of 8 to 10 weeks.

The company's reputation is built on quality and on-time delivery. The Managing Director (MD) is under pressure to maximise the operating profit for the reporting year and honouring the bonus agreement with employees. The two INs focussed their minds on OSH failures and on-time delivery. To comply with the INs, the MD got in touch with an OSH institution, one of his trusted networks. The institution recommended that the company should consult their Directory of OSH consultants and the OSHCR website[58]. However, they were able to give the names of consultant members with expertise in dust extraction systems design and operating within one-hundred-mile radius of the company.

The consultant engaged estimated that the capital cost of a new extraction system using water washing of the extracted dust would be in the order of £30,000. The cost of dismantling and waste management of the old system would entail £7000, and the cost of compressed air supplied RPE (three of it), including training would be in the region of £3000. Two industrial grade vacuum cleaners would cost about £500 each. This meant that the total cost would be about £41,000 plus value added tax (VAT). There would be additional running costs for using LEV, RPE, and a slurry management arrangement.

The MD indicated that, at present, it was not practical to implement the recommendations, deliver the backlog on time and service the refurbishment costs without incurring significant debt, interest payments and putting the company at risk. Their capital reserves were low and would not sustain the proposed costs. The MD and the sales manager were expecting that bookings would accelerate in a few months. So, they asked the OH consultant to come up with an alternative proposal that would enable the company to comply with the INs and deliver their existing orders on time.

The consultant provided an alternative proposal: convert all three open-face receiving hoods into partially enclosing receiving hoods, (an example in Figure 67 below), as recommended in HSE's COSHH Essentials direct advice sheet ST3[158]. The consultant suggested that the partial enclosures could be constructed using fire-retardant wood panels with a suitable access facility for long work items; homemade turntables would be provided and floors marked to show the operator position. These would help efficient extraction of the dust released. Each operator should be provided with a compressed air supplied RPE with a hood and the air quality monitored to conform to BSEN 12021[211]. Two industrial grade vacuum cleaners would be used for regular daily sweeping up any residual dust. Maintaining the cleanliness of the workshop is critical to the recommendations and must be undertaken daily without failure. Before all these controls could be implemented, the whole workshop and the existing extraction system, including the ducts would be subjected to a thorough cleaning using industrial grade vacuum cleaners and RPE. When the financial situation has improved, two 90-degree bends in the LEV system should be straightened as much as is practicable and the dust bagging facility should be upgraded.

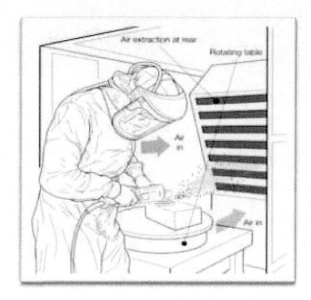

Figure 67[158] An example of a partially enclosing receiving hood.

The estimated cost of the proposed upgrading: thorough cleaning of the system and partially enclosing the receiving hoods system, £2500 to £3000; for the thorough examination, testing, and the TExT report on the upgraded LEV system, £500; providing RPE including training and testing air quality, £3000. One industrial grade vacuum cleaner (for the time being) £500. The total estimated cost would be in the region of £7000.

The MD's worries about timed delivery, not being able to comply with INs, achieving the planned operating profit, upholding the bonus agreement, and the company being put at risk were much reduced by the quick thinking of the OSH consultant. The MD said that the cost of the upgrade could be met from the current cash reserves and a small amount of borrowing, on the expectation that existing orders would be delivered on time and the bookings would accelerate soon.

A respectable OSH-AIDA and a good <u>OSH-RoI</u> from the consultant-related costs.

10.7 Summary

This Chapter introduced and described matters associated with finance related OSH buy-in by operations. They support the technical, legal and social aspects described in the preceding Chapters. The information in this Chapter is based on my personal experience, including limited financial, book-keeping, and accountancy knowledge. Therefore, it is plausible that its accuracy and robustness could be challenged by those with a greater degree of competency in these areas. If that happens to you, invite their help and improve your CPD.

Chapter 11: Make It Happen

"Try not to become a man (person) of success, but rather try to become a man (person) of value (which will include success, prudence, objectivity etc.)"

- Albert Einstein, Theoretical Physicist.

11.1 Introduction

Make it happen: communicate, nudge and influence through your networks - employers, managers, supervisors, buyers, employees, professional colleagues, trade unionists and salespeople. **Don't just rely solely and pin your hopes on RAs, endless checklists, clipboards, and databases; and on recommending RPE, LEV, gloves, ear-defenders, yellow vests, safety hats, boots, and glasses.**

So, I compare Chapters 1-9 of this book with the compartments of a train, Chapter 10 as the driver, and this Chapter as the engine. Without the engine, compartments, however good they may be, cannot do much of the intended jobs, and for the train to move, the driver's hand must be on the 'dead-man' handle. Let's look at an analogy from a human perspective. When we were born, we cried (*communicated*) to *nudge* our mothers for their *attention* and *influenced* them to *think, interpret, react and act* to deliver required solutions.

To make efficient and effective use of the ideas, solutions, suggestions, and examples in the other ten Chapters and your OSHKE, I invite you to maximise the use of communication and nudging techniques. Although the use of risk communication techniques and behavioural science for influencing OSH outcomes is not new to you, influencing or persuading stakeholders for desired OSH behaviours can be challenging and have advantages as well as pitfalls[212]. For us to improve trust, credibility, and acceptance among our stakeholders approaches used for delivering improved OSH outcomes must be seen as fair and just. This Chapter brings together the salient points associated with effective risk communication and nudging for practical applications.

11.2 Basics of communication, Cs in communication and anchoring

The basic elements and concepts involved in communication are summarised in Table 17.

Table 17 Basics of communication, Cs in communication and anchoring

What is Communication? [213]	Cs in communication[214]	Anchoring[130]
It involves: ✓ A sender, ✓ A receiver, ✓ A message(s), ✓ A channel(s), and ✓ (Feedback)	Correct, Complete, Clear, Concise, Credible, Compelling, Considerate, Compassionate, Courteous, and Confident. **These Cs can help you with** *'I can do optimism.'*	**People will remember –** A little of what they hear, Some of what they read, Much of what they see, and Almost all of what they understand fully, practice, and experience.

11.3 Communication and OSH goals

When writing to or addressing an audience, be clear about your OSH goals, because your effective communication is a means to your goals. Listed below are a few pointers.

• What is your purpose in communicating with your audience? If you are not sure, then your audience won't be sure either.

• To be clear, minimise the number of ideas in each sentence or message, but include enough detail.

• Make sure the message is easy for your audience: the meaning, purpose, and intended outcome.

• They shouldn't have to 'read between the lines' and make assumptions on their own to understand what you are trying to say.

• Be concise in your communication, stick to the point and keep it brief.

- Always look out for unnecessary filler words and get rid of them. They don't add substantial value to your communication, instead, they can confuse your message. Examples of filler words include – um, you know, like, basically, really, just, so, and I mean.

- When the message is concrete, complete and concise, your audience should have a clear picture.

Make a note of the three key messages in each of the bullet points in the above list. Using three key messages in communication is a common practice in sales, marketing, and in RM. Recently, it was used effectively in Covid virus-safe messages. You, too, can benefit from the approach; more detail can be found in Table 18 below.

11. 4 Risk Communication

Risk may be defined as uncertainty, whether positive or negative, that will affect the outcome of an activity or an intervention. **Risk communication** may be expressed as an open (honesty in our trade is important) two-way exchange of information and opinion about the harms and benefits of RM. Whereas, **'OSH-spin'** attempts to use/influence communication to sell a specific message/product/service that is heavily biased in favour of the communicator's own requirements and wants. During an OSH-spin, an OSH issue could be 'dressed up' to muddy the reality, cover-up one's incompetency, or confuse and control a situation.

OSHKE

Examine these two plausible statements, analyse, reflect and decide whether they are OSH-spin.

1. An OSH practitioner sells services by persuading an employer to carry out lead-in-air dust exposure monitoring in a wood working shop, where lead-based products/materials were not in use for years. Reasons cited: lead regulations, lead action limits should not be exceeded, and the safety data sheets do not give adequate details.

2. An employer, instead of implementing adequate exposure control measures against wood dust exposure, spins the story - HSE has banned brooms – a diversion to get media publicity, and parts of the media fall for the story.

11.5 OSH-RM communication purposes

OSH communication should aim to:

- Enhance the knowledge and understanding of our audience.

- Build trust and credibility among them.

- Encourage them to adapt appropriate attitudes, behaviours, and beliefs for achieving effective exposure control.

11.6 Key elements involved in effective RM communication

When preparing for effective risk communication activities, the key elements summarised in Table 18 could be used as an aide-memoire. These are based on Covello[215], Sandman[216,217], "UK Resilience"[218] and others[219-225].

Table 18 Key areas to focus during RM communication

Key elements	Linkage
Anticipate, prepare and practice	Anticipate audience wants, needs and fears. These can affect the way they hear, understand, and remember information. Prepare and practice well. Reflect on the OSH-spin examples above.
Messenger	The credibility of the messenger is important to your audience. It comes from the degree of expertise (competency); reputation; organisation represented; position held in relation to the message.
Message	When you have decided your message, address it to believe worthiness (deserving attention) in terms of objectivity, accuracy, and linkage with previous communication on the subject, including HSE's policy and enforcement interests, etc.

3/9/27/140 rule	To help anchoring - limit the number of <u>key messages</u> to a maximum of 3, using a maximum of 27 words (aim for a maximum of 9 words per message), and a total of 140 characters. Each message should take 9 seconds or less to read. Each key message may be augmented by three <u>supporting messages</u> or three credible sources. These can be pictures, personal stories, short videos, references, etc.
Aiming	Construct messages to be easily understood by an adult with year 9 to year 10 education. Because, when concerned about an issue (or in don't-care situations), your audience processes information well below their education level and may concentrate less. (Did you ever let your mind wander during a presentation? – recall some of the reasons).
Risk perception/ outrage/fear factors	Develop your key messages and their supporting information to address what is 'important' to your audience. These may be trust, benefits, personal control, freedom, voluntariness, dread, fairness, catastrophic potential, effects on children, morality, origin, and familiarity.
Risk comparison	Compared with what? - with time (risk decreasing or increasing over a period); against another product, hazard, or method of operation.
Risk framing	The way the message is presented. For example, 1 in 100 workers (or one of you will) die in the construction industry every year (-). (99 of) you go home safely every day, because of the precautions taken by you and the construction industry (+).
Negative vs positive	When your audience 'don't-care' about an OSH situation and/or control solutions or not concerned about the situation, they will focus much more on negative information than positive information. You should construct messages while recognising the dominant role of negative thinking in high concern/don't-care situations. Examples include: avoid unnecessary, indefensible or non-productive use of absolutes (e.g. 90% certain) and words such as – no, not, never, nothing, and none; balance or counter a negative message with a positive, constructive, and solutions-oriented key messages. Provide three positive points to counter a single negative point or bad news. Try and avoid risk framing such as

	'that is not safe,' 'you are ignoring safety,' 'get things right,' etc. It is much more productive to construct positive messages and provide the solution the person would want to use.
Channels of communication	Types used and audience interest in them – magazines, TV, games, roleplay, demonstrations, team meeting, slide presentations, etc.
You care (RUB 4 CCO)	Your audience wants to be convinced that you care before they care about what you know or say. Your audience should Recognise (know from what you say, body language, voice, etc.), Understand and Believe that you care. Galvanise it by enthusing: Compassion, Conviction, and Optimism.
Preamble to the message	Provide a preamble to your message map that indicates genuine empathy, listening, caring, and compassion. These are crucial factors for establishing trust in high-concern, high risk, high stress, don't-care situations.
Primacy/recency	Adhere to the primacy/recency (first/last) principle - what they hear first and last. Most important messages should occupy the first and the last positions. If in their self-interest, they will consider, reflect, and act on your messages.
Information credibility	Cite third parties or sources that would be perceived as credible by your audience. They actively seek out additional information (credible or otherwise).
Aids	Use simple graphics, visual aids, analogies, demonstrations, and narratives (e.g. personal story). These can increase an individual's ability or willingness to hear, understand, and recall a message easily/readily.
Triple T- model	Present your message map using the triple T-model. Tell me; Tell me more; Tell me again.

11.7 Putting into practice – an example risk communication

In one of your training sessions, you are planning to communicate about the importance of LEV hood design and its correct use for the effective extraction of airborne contaminants. In this example, you have decided to use twelve key messages with the help of twelve PowerPoint slides. To help you, I have created the twelve key messages (Table 19), but you may reconstruct them to suit your audiences' needs and wants. To help your thinking, I have provided an example supporting visual for use with the key message 1.

Table 19 An example exercise on effective risk communication

Key Message	Supporting message 1	Supporting message 2	Supporting message 3
1. Lev hood is key to extraction. (Figure 1 in HSG258[127])	Without the hood, LEV is useless.	Hood is where the contaminated air enters the LEV.	Match the hood shape & size. (To the process and the contaminant cloud size.)
2. Position the hood correctly.	Otherwise, inefficient extraction.	Incorrect positioning means, the contaminant escapes into BZ.	Operators will become exposed.
3. Work within the capture zone of the hood.	Hood should generate sufficient airflow at and around the source.	It means the hood can work efficiently.	Operators protected; NHS supported.

OSHKE

Here are examples of key suggestions for you to construct your twelve PowerPoint slides.

Use the key elements in Table 18 as an aide-memoire and consider:

(i) How will you construct your slides *(for example, title, background colour, font, layout, how many words and how)*

(ii) What aids (visuals – pictures, diagrams, videos, Tables, etc.) and how will they support the message?

(iii)What supporting notes/aids will you have to support you?

When you have constructed the presentation, test it out with your friends, and colleagues, and reflect. With their help update and test out your effort as an effective communicator.

11.8 Nudging for influencing better behaviours

Nudging, urging, or channelling is a way of tweaking the choices to influence another's choice without force or threat. The approach involves a 'choice architecture' and the 'choice architect', who designs the choices. Nudging is not new, many of us and animals use it frequently. In essence, it is a form of fine-tuning an action to influence a better behaviour (choices and actions). It can be analysed using Figure 68.

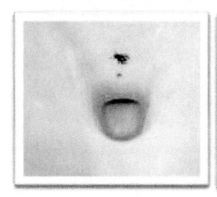 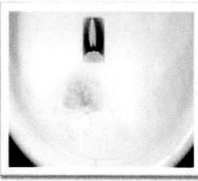

Figure 68 A fly and a lit candle as insets in male urinals.

In this case, as soon as the fly or the lit candle is spotted by the person wanting to use the urinal, the man's automatic desire (thinking) would be to kill the nuisance fly or to put out the fire (depending on which one of the urinals is used). With those desires, the man would aim the stream at the object.

This simple but clever intervention (nudge), in association with urinal design, helped to significantly reduce spillages around urinals. For the facilities management, a smaller number of cleaning routines, reduced use of cleaning chemicals and manpower, reduction in cost centre expenditure; and an improved image of the facility. In terms of OSH, there is a potential for reducing the cleaning related manual handling risks and contact dermatitis caused by regular skin exposure to chemicals and water.

For a nudging intervention to be effective and to win hearts and minds, it should be easy to adopt without coercion and be cost effective. The Nobel prize winning Professor Thaler and his colleague Professor Sunstein[219-221] described nudge as: any aspect of the choice architecture that alters people's behaviour in a predictable way without forbidding any options or significantly changing their economic incentives.

Nudges are not mandates like the requirements of COSHH regulations 6: **"An employer shall not carry out work which is liable to expose any employees to any substance hazardous**

to health unless he has— (a) made a suitable and sufficient assessment of the risk created by that work to the health of those employees and of the steps that need to be taken to meet the requirements of these Regulations."

Nudges are choices by design, for example, installing a timed auto-release lock to a LEV enclosure door on a Computer Numerical Control (CNC) drilling/cutting/boring machine and linking the operation of the switch to the metal working fluid mist clearance time for that hood. CNC machine operators are unlikely to force open the door before auto-release or install and use a bypass switch to beat the timed auto-release. The nudge in this scenario is simple, easy and cheap for the operators (as well as employers) to adopt as a default choice. In summary, a nudge approach should be[219-222]:

- Transparent and not misleading.

- Easy as possible to opt out of the nudge.

- About the belief that the act/choice/behaviour being encouraged will improve the welfare of those being nudged.

- Associated with technical, procedural, and organisational measures rather than purely psychological ones.

I shall explain nudging in another way because it is an important tool in our toolbox. Your ability to influence attitudes and behaviours (of directors, managers, supervisors, employees, safety representatives, etc.) is essential to your efforts on OSH-RM. As you know, the usual route is to focus on attempting to 'change minds' by influencing the way your target audience think through information, such as training on COSHH regulations, RAs and PPE. There is, however, evidence to show that 'changing contexts'[223-225], by influencing the environment in which operatives work and managers act, can have significant positive effects on behaviour. In other words, situations we find ourselves in, like the urinal example in Figure 68 and the CNC machine example, have a significant influence. Although decision-making is complex, because of the situations individuals find themselves in, the target audience do the intended act largely automatically and without extensive thinking, reflection, and analysis. In other words, they act through their 'automatic mind' ('**system 1 mind**') rather than their 'analytical mind' ('**system 2** mind')[223-225]. A brief comparative summary and a simplified pictorial representation of the ways in which these two minds function are presented below.

- The functioning of system 1 is automatic, uncontrolled, effortless, associative, fast, unconscious, emotional, and error prone.

- Whereas system 2 is reflective, deliberative, more logical, controlled, effortful, rule-based, slow, conscious, makes rational and 'reliable' decisions.

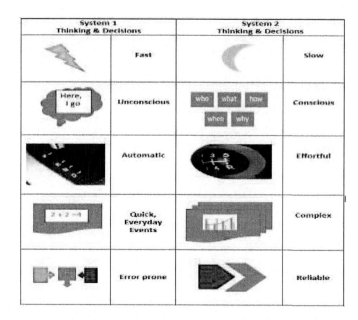

Figure 69 Functioning of System 1 and System 2 minds, a pictorial illustration.

174

It is considered that a carefully thought-out ways to harness the decision-making ability of the automatic mind can have advantages in OSH-RM activities. In that context, consider the salient points in Table 20, explained using the 'MINDSPACE' framework[222]. It is a mnemonic to explain the nine influences (Table 20) on human behaviour. They have been used to explain and intervene in various subject areas, including OSH. The MINDSPACE framework helps to maximise the usefulness of Kahneman's System1/System2 thinking[224] and the nudge theory explained by Thaler and Sunstein[219-221]. In summary, MINDSPACE explores how our behaviours can be shaped and influenced.

Table 20 MINDSPACE[222].

Messenger 	**We are heavily influenced by who communicates information to us.** *In this case, the mother elephant is trusted as a compassionate, considerate and believable messenger.* *The baby elephant is likely to act automatically on the message(s) given by the mother. The baby may nudge her mother to an action too.* In OSH, HSE is generally considered as a trusted, believable and considerate messenger.
Incentives 	**Our responses to incentives are shaped by predictable mental shortcuts to avoid losses.** *Drivers' behaviours get moderated by the camera. Incentives include avoiding speeding fines, points on licence, and the potentials such as increased insurance premium. In this case, no one will think of the Traffic Act or whether the camera has a film.* Using safety barrier systems, auto-release locks, signs, marking LEV hoods capture zones are OSH examples.
Norms 	**We are strongly influenced by what others do.** *The visual 'No Entry' sign acted as a norm/default. A suitable line was formed on the intended side, a safe distance maintained, and masks worn.* Most operatives would wear RPE in a RPE zone indicated by a suitable visual sign and need communicated with RPE wearers' interests, not saying COSHH requires you to wear RPE.
Defaults	**We go with the flow of pre-set options.** *Drivers' choices and actions are managed by the lane markings. Most would choose the right one for them.* Using 'dead-man' trigger on a sandblasting nozzle instead of taping it up to defeat the safety system.

Salience	**Our attention is drawn to what is novel and seems relevant to us.** *Modern air fryers are helping with our desire to consume less fat and electricity.* Workplace examples include welding torch with on-tool extraction, low fume welding electrodes, vacuum drying wet components, and respirators fitted with automatic volume flow control to cope with the breathing rate of the wearer.
Priming 	**Our acts are often influenced by sub-conscious cues.** Professor Reason's cheese model picture as a computer screen saver would make OHS practitioners automatically think about the need for error management and taking measures to control the weaknesses in RM measures.
Affection 	**Our emotional associations can powerfully shape our actions.** *Don't we all love the cuddle and affection from those close to us? Most of us will not wilfully go against them.* Workers should feel that the OHS-RM efforts are genuine and they can trust and believe that it is in their interest. We have read about "danger money', where negative nudging played an important part (Section 3.10, Chapter 3).
Commitments	**We seek to be consistent with our public promises and reciprocal acts.** *Wedding rings are a powerful symbol of our commitments and reciprocal actions.* OHS-RM measures should be easy to use, and everyone in a section should sign-up. The measures should be easy to use, not misleading, not seen as a measure for punishment. They should deliver beyond the "safety first" cliché. It is important to consult operatives when OSH measures are planned and implemented.
Ego	**We act in ways that make us feel better about ourselves.** *Fancy sunglasses and a seaside holiday in a warm place, in this example. I have earnt it, I deserve it, etc.* Innovations in safety eyewear have made a significant difference in worker acceptability and eye protection, leading to a significantly reduced number of eye injuries.

OSHKE

Communication and Nudging. As an OSH practitioner, create a practically based risk communication approach to nudge <u>self-employed</u> paving workers for controlling their exposure to crystalline silica containing dust. Many of these individuals are lone and transient workers and carry out open-air block paving jobs. When constructing your risk communication message, take account of all the points learnt so far.

Facts: From 1 October 2015, if self-employed and their work activity poses no potential risk to the OSH of other workers or members of the public, then health and safety law will not apply.

Assumptions: (i) Self-employed persons in this case study are not causing silica dust exposure risk to others (no other workers or public in the close vicinity); (ii) Dry cutting is predominant; (iii) Use second hand equipment bought at auctions; (iv) Don't have access to piped running water; (v) Regularly buy replacement saw blades at trade counters of nationally based outfits.

If you are unfamiliar with stone cutting, watch the video <u>before doing the exercise - 6 Ways to Cut a Paving Stone - Bing video</u>

Key Messages: Here is a thought to fire your imagination. Message 1. **Wear mask.** Message 2. **Silica dust causes lung cancer.** Message 3. **Save hard pressed NHS & your lungs.**

Practical thoughts: Is it hard for them to have a small water butt on board their pickup trucks, which can be used for gravity feeding their power cutting tools and including the cost of a disposable RPE in their contract price.

11.9 Summary

This chapter introduced many salient points, examples and exercises on effective risk communication and nudging. They should help you to maximise individual, social, technological, financial and other work contexts for positively influencing behaviours in OSH-RM situations. The approaches introduced in this Chapter are not new and have been successfully applied in OSH, commercial, marketing, and public policy developments. For those new to the art of effective risk communication and nudging, it remains for you to apply them, as appropriate, in your workplace context.

Concluding remarks

In my mind's eye, I have done the deed to deliver my two aims for this book.

- *Helping to make your job easy, and*

- *Helping you to engage, explain, encourage and positively nudge 'colleagues' to improve exposure control decision making.*

I sincerely hope that the contents of this book will, in small ways, help to counter-claim myths among some quarters that OSH legislation is to blame for preventing business activities.

It remains to say, my good wishes to you for delivering effective and efficient OSH leadership (engage, explain, encourage) and to help employers achieve OSH protection for people at work and making money.

In my thoughts of praise, your efforts must be to mirror the vision of Lao Tzu, an ancient Chinese Philosopher, and Poet - 'A leader is best when people barely know he exists, when his work is done, his aim is fulfilled, they will say: we did it ourselves.'

References

(Accessibility retested on 7 November 2022)

1. Oxford University Press. (2022) Oxford Reference: Hippocrates. Hippocrates - Oxford Reference

2. Harvard Public Health. (2017) Airs, Waters, and Places: A climate Change Series. Airs, Waters, and Places: A Climate Change Series | Harvard Public Health Magazine | Harvard T.H. Chan School of Public Health

3. Carnevale F, Lavicoli s. (2015) Bernardo Ramazzini (1633-1714): A visionary physician, scientist and communicator. Occup Environ Med; 72:1-3. Bernardino Ramazzini (1633–1714): a visionary physician, scientist and communicator | Occupational & Environmental Medicine (bmj.com)

4. Encyclopidia.com (2016) Bernardino Ramazzini. Bernardini Ramazzini | Encyclopedia.com

5. Franco G, Franco F. (2001) Diseases of the Workers. American J Public Health; 91: 1380–1382. (PDF) Bernardino Ramazzini: The Father of Occupational Medicine | Franco Franco - Academia.edu

6. Wikipedia (2020) Factory inspector. Factory inspector - Wikipedia

7. Reed S, Pisaniello D, Benke G, Burton K (Editors). (2013) Principles of Occupational Health and Hygiene. Australian Institute of Occupational Hygiene (AIOH) and Allen & Unwin.

8. National Geographic Society. Industrialization, labor, and society. https://www.nationalgeographic.org/article/industrialization-labor-and-life/7th-grade/

9. Craig G, Gaus A, Wilkinson M, Skrivankova K, McQuade A. (2007) Modern Slavery in the United Kingdom. Joseph Rowntree Foundation. Modern slavery in the United Kingdom | JRF

10. Szreter s. (2004) Industrialization and health. Br. Med. Bul; 69: 75-86. https://doi.org/10.1093/bmb/ldh005

11. Dajang TK. (1942) Factory Inspection in Great Britain. George Alan and Unwin Ltd, London. Factory inspection in Great Britain (1942 edition) | Open Library Also at:

Piney M. (2001) (PDF) The development of chemical exposure limits for the workplace. (researchgate.net)

12. Internet Archive. (2021) Second report of the Departmental Committee appointed to inquire into the ventilation of factories and workshops. Pt. 1, Report: Great Britain. Home Office. Committee on Ventilation of Factories and Workshops : Free Download, Borrow, and Streaming: Internet Archive

13. Ogden TL. (2003) Commentary: The 1968 BOHS Chrysotile standard. Ann Occup Hyg; 47:3-6. https://doi.org/10.1093/annhyg/meg011

14. The National Archives (Legislation-UK). Factories Act 1937. Factories Act 1937 (legislation.gov.uk)

15. Isaac P (Ed). (1993) First forty years: Account of the formation and the development of the British Occupational Hygiene Society (BOHS), 1953-93. (Access via: BOHS).

16. Cherrie JW. (2003) Commentary: The beginning of the science underpinning occupational hygiene. Ann Occup Hyg; 47:179-185. https://doi.org/10.1093/annhyg/meg030

17. Ogden T. (2006) Annals of Occupational Hygiene at Volume 50: Many achievements, a few mistakes and an interesting future. Ann Occup Hyg; 50:751-764. https://doi.org/10.1093/annhyg/mel070

18. BOHS. (2013) BOHS - 60 years (1953-2013): A healthy working environment for everyone. British Occupational Hygiene Society.

19. The National Archives (Legislation-UK- HSWA.) Health and Safety at Work etc. Act 1974. Health and Safety at Work etc. Act 1974 (legislation.gov.uk)

20. HSE 49. (2013) A guide to health and safety regulation in Great Britain HSE49

21. Legislation-UK. (2021-COSHH) COSHH. The Control of Substances Hazardous to Health Regulations 1988 (legislation.gov.uk).

22. Health and Safety Executive (HSE-L5). (2013) Control of substances Hazardous to health. Control of substances hazardous to health (COSHH). The Control of Substances Hazardous to Health Regulations 2002 (as amended). Approved Code of Practice and guidance L5 (hse.gov.uk).

23. Mellor A. (2020) Be amazing – Go home healthy. https://youtu.be/NLxq2HcwLN4

24. HSE (CLP). (2009) Chemical classification: The GB CLP Regulation (hse.gov.uk)

25. HSE (EH40). (2005) EH40/2005 Workplace exposure limits (hse.gov.uk)

26. BOHS - dust trigger values (2021) Information for BOHS members on application of COSHH to dust not assigned Workplace Exposure Limits or hazard classifications, and on application of good control practice. Low-Toxicity-Dusts-and-Good-Control-Practice-11_08_21.pdf (bohs.org)

27. Cherrie JW, Brosseau LM, Hay A and Donaldson K. (2013). Low-toxicity dusts: Current exposure guideline are not sufficiently protective. Ann Occup Hyg; 57: 681-689. 10.1093/annhyg/met038

28. Trade Union Congress. (2011) Dust in the workplace. Dust in the Workplace | TUCregulatory

29. Tran CL, Miller BG, Jones AD. (2003). Risk assessment of inhaled particles using a physiologically based mechanistic model. HSE Research Report 141. Institute of Occupational Medicine. Edinburgh. RR141 - Risk assessment of inhaled particles using a physiologically based mechanistic model (hse.gov.uk)

30. HSE (Webpage). Is there a specific amount of dust that can be hazardous to health? Health and Safety Executive. FAQs - Dust - HSE

31. BOHS/Netherlands Occupational Hygiene Society. (2011) Testing compliance with occupational exposure limits for airborne substances. 2011-12-bohs-nvva-sampling-strategy-guidance.pdf (arbeidshygiene.nl).

32. HSE. (2012) Control of diesel engine exhaust emissions in the workplace (HSG187). Control of diesel engine exhaust emissions in the workplace (hse.gov.uk)

33. Cooke J, Simpson A, Yates T and Llewellyn D. (2017) Exposure to substances hazardous to health in foundries. rr1115.pdf (hse.gov.uk)

34. The National Archives. The Management of Health and Safety at Work Regulations 1999 (legislation.gov.uk)

35. Creely KS, Van Tongeren, While D. et.al. (2006) Trends in inhalation exposure. HSE Research Report. Institute of Occupational Medicine. RR460 - Trends in inhalation exposure mid 1980s till present (hse.gov.uk)

36. HSE. (2021). Self-reported lung problems. Occupational Lung Disease statistics in Great Britain, 2020 (hse.gov.uk)

37. HSE-skin. (2021) Work-related Skin disease. Work-related skin disease statistics in Great Britain, 2020 (hse.gov.uk)

38. HSE-asthma. (2021). Work-related asthma Statistics. Work-related asthma statistics in Great Britain, 2020 (hse.gov.uk)

39. HSE-cancer. (2021) Occupational cancer statistics. Occupational Cancer statistics in Great Britain, 2020 (hse.gov.uk)

40. Cancer Research UK. (2021) Cancer statistics for the UK. Cancer Statistics for the UK (cancerresearchuk.org)

41. Public Health England. (2019) Guidance -Health matters: health and work. Health matters: health and work - GOV.UK (www.gov.uk)

42. HSE. (2022) Public register of enforcement notices. Public register of enforcement notices (hse.gov.uk).

43. HSE. (2022) Register of convictions and notices. HSE - Register of prosecutions and notices.

44. LÖftstedt RE. (2011) Reclaiming health and safety for all: an independent review of health and safety regulations. Reclaiming health and safety for all: An independent review of health and safety legislation (publishing.service.gov.uk)

45. Oxford Learner's Dictionaries. (2021) Proportionality. proportionality noun - Definition, pictures, pronunciation and usage notes | Oxford Advanced Learner's Dictionary at OxfordLearnersDictionaries.com

46. Regulatory Policy Committee (UK). Proportionality guidance for departments and regulators. Final_proportionality_.pdf (publishing.service.gov.uk)

47. Lam R. (2021) Proportionality vs Rationality Review: A False Dichotomy. King's Student Law Review. Proportionality vs Rationality Review: A False Dichotomy? – Rachelle Lam – King's Student Law Review (kcl.ac.uk)

48. HSE. (2001) Reducing risks, protecting people: HSE's decision-making process (2001). Reducing Risks: Protecting People - HSE's decision making process

49. HSE. (2015) Enforcement policy statement (v1). DRAFT Enforcement Policy Statement (hse.gov.uk)

50. HSE. (2013) Enforcement management model (EMM): Operational version V3.2. Enforcement Management Model - Operational (hse.gov.uk)

51. HSE. (2001) Reducing Risks: Protecting People - HSE's decision making process

52. Risk and Regulation Advisory Council. (2009) Health and Safety in small organisations (2009). www.bis.gov.uk/files/file52340.pdf

53. Young DI. (2010) Common Sense Common Safety. Common Sense, Common Safety (publishing.service.gov.uk)

54. HSE. (2019) Understanding the impact of business-to-business health and safety 'rules.' Understanding the impact of business to business health and safety 'rules' (hse.gov.uk)

55. HSE (webpage). Insight research reports. Insight research (hse.gov.uk)

56. Bevan J. (2020) Exploring and tackling business to business safety 'rules.' HSE. PowerPoint Presentation (iosh.com)

57. HSE (webpage). Health and safety accreditation schemes. Health and safety accreditation schemes - Competence in health and safety (hse.gov.uk)

58. Occupational Safety and Health Consultants Register (OSHCR). Find a safety and health expert. Health & Safety Consultants | Occupational H&S Register (oshcr.org)

59. Government Legal Department. (2022) "The Judge Over Your Shoulder" - GOV.UK (www.gov.uk)

60. HSE (1993) COSHH-the HSE's 1991/92 evaluation survey. Occupational Health Review 44, 10-15. (Out of print, a summary can be seen in reference 62).

61. Biggs D, Crumbie N. (2000) The characteristics of people working with chemical products in small firms. HSE Contract Research Report 278/2000. https://www.hse.gov.uk/research/crr_pdf/2000/crr00278.pdf

62. Topping MD, Williams CR, Devine JM. (1998) Industry's perception and use of occupational exposure limits. Ann Occup Hyg; 42: 357–66. PII: S0003-4878(98)00054-4 (cdc.gov)

63. Hudspith B, Hay AWM. (1998) Information needs of workers. Ann Occup Hyg; 42: 401–6. https://doi.org/10.1093/annhyg/42.6.401

64. Tijssen SCHA, Links IHM. (2002) Ways for SMEs to assess and control risks from hazardous substances. HSE Research Report 014/2001. TNO-Environmental Toxicology, The Netherlands. RR014 - Ways for SMEs to assess and control risks from hazardous substances (hse.gov.uk)

65. Gervais RL, Greaves G, Lekka C. (2008) Hazardous substances at work: findings from focus groups assessing operational staff's, dutyholders' and consultants' perceptions of COSHH, CLAW and DSEAR. HSE Research Report 1125. rr1125.pdf (hse.gov.uk)

66. Rajan R. (1991) Solutions for Safety at Work (S-SAW). Institute of Naval Medicine. Portsmouth. Personal Communication.

67. Gardner RJ, Oldershaw PJ. (1991) Development of pragmatic exposure -control concentrations based on packaging regulations risk phrases. Ann Occup. Hyg; 35: 51-60. https://doi.org/10.1093/annhyg/35.1.51

68. Chemical Industries Association (1992) Safe Handling of Potentially carcinogenic Aromatic Amines and Nitro Compounds. Safe handling of potentially carcinogenic aromatic amines and nitro compounds. (1992 edition) | Open Library

69. Money CD. (1992). A structured approach to occupational hygiene in the design and operation of fine chemical plant. Ann. Occup. Hyg. 36, 601-607. https://doi.org/10.1093/annhyg/36.6.601

70. Money CD. (1992b). The European Chemicals industry's needs and expectations for workplace exposure data. App Occup Env Hyg; 16:300-303. 10.1080/10473220121217

71. Chemical Industries Association (1993). Safe Handling of Colourants 2. Chemical Industries Association. Safe handling of colourants. (1993 edition) | Open Library

72. Guest I (1997) Chemical Industries Association (1997). The Chemicals Industries Association guidance on Allocating Occupational Exposure Bands. Ann Occup Hyg; 42: 407-411. https://doi.org/10.1016/S0003-4878(98)00051-9

73. HSE. (2001) Principles and guidelines to assist HSE in its judgements that duty-holders have reduced risk as low as is reasonably practicable. Health and Safety Executive. Risk management: Expert guidance - Principles and guidelines to assist HSE

74. Elliott C, Appleby M. (2011) Legislation and proportionality – Reckoning with risk. Safety and Health Practitioner (SHP). Legislation and proportionality - Reckoning with risk - SHP - Health and Safety News, Legislation, PPE, CPD and Resources (shponline.co.uk)

75. Authority of the House of Lords Select Committee on Economic Affairs. (2006) Government Policy on the management of risk. Microsoft Word - FINAL REPORT - government policy on the management of risk... (parliament.uk)

185

76. Authority of the House of Commons. (2008) The role of the Health and Safety Commission and the Health and Safety Executive in regulating workplace health and safety (HC246). Microsoft Word - final CRC.doc (parliament.uk)

77. HSE. (2021-statistics) Health and safety at work: Summary statistics for Great Britain 2021. Health and Safety Executive. Health and safety statistics 2021 (hse.gov.uk)

78. HSE (webpage). Cost benefit analysis (CBA) checklist. Health and Safety Executive. Risk management: Expert guidance - Cost Benefit Analysis (CBA) checklist (hse.gov.uk)

79. HSE. (2021-lungs) HSE inspections focus on occupational lung disease, 4 May 2021. Health and Safety Executive inspections focus on occupational lung disease - HSE Media Centre. 4 may 2021. HSE press release (time limited availability), (Accessed:16 August 2021). Alternative: Prevent work-related lung disease - HSE

80. HSE. (2020) HSE cracks down on dust. Health and Safety Executive cracks down on dust - HSE Media Centre. 24 September 2020. HSE press release (time limited availability Accessed: 16 August 2021).

81. HSE. (2022) Health and safety executive supports workers' health at Great Britain's construction sites. Health and Safety Executive supports workers' health at Great Britain's construction sites | HSE Media Centre

82. HSE. (2019). Change in Enforcement Expectations for Mild Steel Welding Fume (hse.gov.uk)

83. HSE. (2022). South Yorkshire businesses targeted for health and safety inspection | HSE Media Centre

84. HSE (webpage) Enforcement Management Model (EMM): Application to Health Risks (hse.gov.uk)

85. The National Archives. Ejector seat manufacturer fined £800,00 for failing to protect workers' health. [ARCHIVED CONTENT] Ejector seat manufacturer fined £800,000 for failing to protect workers' health | Media centre - HSE (nationalarchives.gov.uk).

86. SHP. (2006) Photo firm fined over allergic dermatitis. https://www.shponline.co.uk/chemical-hazards/photo-firm-fined-over-allergic-dermatitis. Company fined after employees suffer from dermatitis - COSHH (hse.gov.uk)

87. Anastas PT, Warner JC. (2000) in Green Chemistry, theory and Practice. Oxford University Press, London. (Out of print). See: Schulte. PA, Mckernan LT, Heidel DS et

al. Occupational safety and health, green chemistry, and sustainability: A review of areas of convergence Env. Health;12 (2013): Article No.31. https://doi.org/10.1186/1476-069X-12-31 and Marshall E. An introduction to green chemistry. Slide 1 (ic.ac.uk)

88. HSE (webpage). Soldering and Asthma. Solderer develops asthma at large manufacturers in Gloucester (hse.gov.uk)

89. HSE (webpage). Allergic contact dermatitis and metal working fluid. Automotive engineering company sentenced after employee has allergic reaction at work - HSE Media Centre. (Time limited availability). Accessed: 16 August 2021. Engineering Company Fined for Metalworking Fluid Exposure (autoextract.co.uk)

90. HSM-Health and Safety Matters (webpage) 12 July 2021 HSM - £360k fine after apprentices suffer chemical burns (hsmsearch.com)

91. HSE (webpage). Prevent work-related lung disease. Prevent work-related lung disease - HSE.

92. HSE (webpage). Direct advice sheets. Direct advice sheets - COSHH e-tool (hse.gov.uk)

93. Tijssen SCHA, Links IHM. (2002) Ways for SMEs to assess and control risks from hazardous substances. HSE Research Report 14. TNO-Environmental Toxicology. (2017) RR014 - Ways for SMEs to assess and control risks from hazardous substances (hse.gov.uk)

94. HSE. COSHH Essentials: Controlling exposure to chemicals – a simple control banding approach. coshh-technical-basis.pdf (hse.gov.uk)

95. Brooke I. (1998) An introduction to a UK scheme to help small firms control health risks from chemical: toxicological considerations. Ann Occup Hyg; 42: 377-390. https://doi.org/10.1016/S0003-4878(98)00050-7

96. Maidment SC. (1998) Occupational hygiene considerations in the development of a structured approach to select chemical control strategies. Ann Occup Hyg; 24: 391-398. https://doi.org/10.1016/S0003-4878(98)00049-0

97. Garrod AN Rajan-Sithamparanadarajah R. (2003) Developing COSHH Essentials: dermal exposure, personal protective equipment and first aid. Ann Occup Hyg; 47: 577-588. https://doi.org/10.1093/annhyg/meg089

98. Vaughan NP, Rajan-Sithamparanadarajah R. (2017) An assessment of the robustness of the COSHH-Essentials (C-E) target airborne concentration ranges 15 years on, and their

usefulness for determining control measures. Ann Work Exp Health; 61: 270-283. https://doi.org/10.1093/annweh/wxx002

99. British Standards Institution (BSI). (2001) Selection, use and maintenance of chemical protective clothing (BS7184). Buy at: BSI - BS 7184 - Selection, Use and Maintenance of Chemical Protective Clothing - Guidance | Engineering360 (globalspec.com)

100. Vaughan N, Rajan-Sithamparanadarajah B, Atkinson R. (2016) Evaluation of RPE-Select: A web-based respiratory protective equipment selector tool. Ann Occup Hyg; 60: 900-912. https://doi.org/10.1093/annhyg/mew035

101. Bates S, Greaves D. (2009) Improving the usefulness of guidance for duty holders. HSE Research Report 737. Health and Safety Laboratory. COSHH and current practice (hse.gov.uk)

102. Ferguson E, Bibby PA, Leavis J and Weyman A. (2003) Effective design of workplace risk communications. HSE Research Report 93). University of Nottingham and Health and Safety Laboratory. RR093 - Effective design of workplace risk communications (hse.gov.uk)

103. Creely KS, Leith s, Graham MK et al. (2003) Effective communication of chemical hazards and risk information using multimedia safety data sheet. HSE Research Report 72. University of Aberdeen. RR072 - Effective communication of chemical hazard and risk information using a multimedia safety data sheet (hse.gov.uk)

104. Price Water House (Comms Lab.). (2017) The power of visual communication. Showing your story to land the message. (PWC). The Power of Visual Communication (pwc.com.au)

105. Gentry A, Barrett C, Hurst C, et.al. (2015) Exposure to isocyanate particles and occupational asthma. Motor Vehicle Repair Studies Department, South Essex College. Exposure to isocyanate particles and occupational asthma in the motor vehicle refinishing industry

106. Din A, Conner B, Hassam H, Jackson M. COSHH & LOcHER Trader. (2020) MVV Environment Baldovie Waste Ltd. COSHH boardgame (safetygroupsuk.org.uk)

107. Kennedy K, Cook M, Hartley D. Dust n' Boots. (2017) Construction Department, Blackpool and the Fylde College. Dust n' Boots - YouTube

108. Fishwick D. How do our Lungs Work? (2020) Learning Occupational Health by Experiencing Risks (LOcHER). How do our lungs work? - YouTube

109. Gadd S, Keely D, Balmforth H. (2003) Good practice and pitfalls in risk assessment. HSE Research Report RR151. HSE. RR151 - Good practice and pitfalls in risk assessment (hse.gov.uk)

110. Bell N, Goodwill E, Whitehouse V, Greaves D. (2018) Hazardous substances at work survey. HSE Research Report 1124. HSE. RR1124 - Hazardous substances at work survey: an analysis of respondents' experiences and views of COSHH, CLAW and DSEAR (hse.gov.uk)

111. HSE (webpage). Busting the health and safety myths. Busting the health and safety myths (hse.gov.uk)

112. HSE (webpage). Work-related fatal injuries in GB. Statistics - Work-related fatal injuries in Great Britain (hse.gov.uk)

113. HSE (webpage). Statistics - Work-related ill health and occupational disease (hse.gov.uk)

114. HSE (webpage). Health surveillance and occupational health - HSE

115. HSE-HS asthma questionnaire. Health questionnaire for on-going surveillance of people potentially exposed to substances that can cause occupational asthma. HSE's Health questionnaire

116. University of Cambridge. (2018) Staff working with Respiratory/Skin Sensitisers – Initial Assessment. UNIVERSITY OF CAMBRIDGE

117. University of Edinburgh. (2018) Skin surveillance questionnaire. skin surveillance questionnaire

118. NHS. (2018) Skin surveillance questionnaire. skin surveillance questionnaire

119. HSE (webpage). Cost to Great Britain of workplace injuries and new cases of work-related ill health-2018/19. Health and Safety Executive. Statistics - Costs to Britain of workplace injuries and new cases of work-related ill health (hse.gov.uk)

120. HSE (webpage). COSHH Case studies. Case studies - COSHH (hse.gov.uk)

121. Scottish Healthy Working Lives (webpage). Self assessments. Self assessments - Healthy Working Lives

122. HSE (webpage) ISO 45001 health and safety management standard. ISO 45001 Health and safety management standard - HSE

123. Office for National Statistics. (2022) EM14: Employees and self-employed by industry. EMP14: Employees and self-employed by industry - Office for National Statistics (ons.gov.uk)

124. HSE (webpage). Transient workers. Transient workers (hse.gov.uk)

125. Alcumus. (2019) COSHH Management: How UK Businesses are managing the challenge. Industry Plant and Equipment (IPE). IPE - COSHH Management: How UK Businesses are managing the challenge (ipesearch.co.uk)

126. Fairman R, Yapp C. (2005) Making an impact on SME compliance behaviour. HSE Research Report 366. Kings College, University of London. RR366 - Making an impact on SME compliance behaviour: An evaluation of the effect of intervention upon compliance with Health and Safety legislation in small and medium sized enterprises. (hse.gov.uk)

127. HSE. (2017) Controlling airborne contaminants at work: A guide to local exhaust ventilation (LEV, HSG258). Controlling airborne contaminants at work: A guide to local exhaust ventilation (LEV) - HSG258 (hse.gov.uk)

128. Fidderman H, McDonnell K. RoSPA. (2010). Worker involvement in health and safety: what works? Royal Society for Prevention of Accidents (RoSPA). Worker involvement in health and safety: what works? (hse.gov.uk)

129. HSE (webpage). Consulting your employees. https://www.hse.gov.uk/toolbox/managing/consulting.htm

130. Sithamparanadarajah R. (2008) Controlling skin exposure to chemicals and wet-work. BOHS/RMS publication (Out of print).

131. HSE (1999) Reducing errors and influencing behaviours (HSG48). HSE. hsg48.pdf (hse.gov.uk)

132. Rajan B. (2022) 'Danger money.' Personal communication.

133. Bell N, Vaughan NP, Morris L and Griffin P. (2012) An assessment of workplace programmes designed to control inhalational risks using respiratory protective equipment. Ann work exp and health; 56: 350-361. https://doi.org/10.1093/annhyg/mer109

134. HSE (webpage). Case studies: when leadership falls short. https://www.hse.gov.uk/leadership/casestudies-failures.htm

135. HSE (2022) Health priority plan: Occupational lung disease. Health and Safety Executive. occupational-lung-disease.pdf (hse.gov.uk) (Accessed on 5 May 2022, now withdrawn).

136. Safety Groups UK (SGUK). Learning Occupational Health by Experiencing Risks (LOcHER). LOcHER (safetygroupsuk.org.uk)

137. Rajan R. (1990) There are no side effects when using paints. Personal communication.

138. Smith R, Kelly A. (2016) Workers' perspectives and preferences for learning across working life in 'Supporting learning across working life.' 10.1007/978-3-319-29019-5_12

139. National Centre for Social Research. (2010) How best to communicate health and safety messages to young learners in vocational education and training. HSE Research Report 803. HSE. How best to communicate health and safety messages to young learners in vocational education and training (hse.gov.uk)

140. Lekka C, Bennet V. (2014) Literature review: Understanding how to improve the management of exposure to wood dust amongst construction sub-contractors and manufacturing SMEs. HSE Research Report RR1017. Health and Safety Laboratory. Microsoft Word - ph08147_ww lit search_approved report.doc (hse.gov.uk)

141. Rajan B, MacDonell K, Foy D. (2020) Essential steps to safe working with substances hazardous to health. locher-coshh-poster-with-author-names.jpg (1754×2480) (safetygroupsuk.org.uk)

142. Rajan B. (2021) COSHH Basics. COSHH Basics (safetygroupsuk.org.uk)

143. Rajan B. (2021) Health risks control online modules, LOcHER. Health Risks Control Online Modules (safetygroupsuk.org.uk)

144. ARCO/SGUK/LOcHER (2021) A simple dashboard on risk assessment and risk management. sr-2322-locher-risk-assessment-dashboard-v2-1.pdf (safetygroupsuk.org.uk)

145. Scottish Centre for Healthy Working Lives. (2009) Health Risks at Work. Do You Know Yours? Health Risks at Work (healthyworkinglives.scot)

146. Appuhamy R. (2018) Risk and how to use a risk matrix. https://youtu.be/-E-jfcoR2W0

147. HSE-CIS54. (2010) Dust control on cut-off saws used for stone or concrete cutting. CIS54 - Dust control on cut-off saws used for stone or concrete cutting (hse.gov.uk)

148. HSE. (2016) Cutting blocks, paving and kerb stones with a cut-off saw-CN6. COSHH essentials: CN6: Cutting blocks, paving and kerbstones with a cut-off saw (hse.gov.uk)

149. HSE. (2021) Welding fume control (WL3). wl3.pdf (hse.gov.uk)

150. Slater M. (2010) Managing LEV systems – have things improved. Diamond Environmental Ltd. Managing LEV systems – have things improved? – Recognition, Evaluation, Control (wordpress.com)

151. Slater M. (2011) Risk management measures in the real world. Diamond Environmental Ltd. Risk Management Measures in the real world – Recognition, Evaluation, Control (wordpress.com)

152. Slater M. (2010a). What's wrong with captor hoods. Diamond Environmental Ltd. What's wrong with captor hoods? – Recognition, Evaluation, Control (wordpress.com)

153. HSE. (2016) Bag opening, tipping and dough mixing. FL1 Bag opening, tipping and dough mixing (hse.gov.uk)

154. HSE. LEV and wood dust. https://www.hse.gov.uk/construction/healthrisks/hazardous-substances/wood-cutting-uncontrolled.mp4

155. HSE. (2020) Cross cut saw (direct advice sheet, WD3). wd3.pdf (hse.gov.uk)

156. HSE. Wood dust control and LEV. https://www.hse.gov.uk/construction/healthrisks/hazardous-substances/wood-cutting-controlled.mp4

157. Dobbie J, Thomson E. (2014) Joint IOSH/BOHS control event- Local Exhaust Ventilation Demo. BOHS.

158. HSE. (2022) Cutting and polishing using hand-held rotary tools (Direct advice sheet). st3.pdf (hse.gov.uk)

159. Lee, EG, Slaven J, Bowen, R et. al. (2011) Evaluation of the COSHH Essentials model with a mixture of organic chemicals at a medium-sized pain t producer. Ann Occup Hyg; 55:16-29. https://doi.org/10.1093/annhyg/meq067

160. Zalk DM, West E, Nelson DI (2021). Control banding: Background, evolution, and application. Patty's Industrial Hygiene. Control Banding: Background, Evolution, and Application - Zalk - Major Reference Works - Wiley Online Library

161. Tischer M, Bredendiek-Kampher S, Poppek U. (2003) Evaluation of the HSE COSHH-Essentials Exposure predictive model on the basis of BAuA field studies and existing

substance exposure database. Ann Occup Hyg; 47: 559-69. https://doi.org/10.1093/annhyg/meg086

162. Jones RM, Nicas M. (2006) Evaluation of COSHH Essentials for vapour degreasing and bag filling operations. Ann Occup Hyg;50: 137-147. 10.1093/annhyg/mei053

163. Money C, Bailey s, Smith M, et. al. (2006) Evaluation of the utility and reliability of COSHH Essentials. Ann Occup Hyg. 2006 50: 642-644. https://doi.org/10.1093/annhyg/mel044

164. Hashimoto H, Goto T, Nakachi N et al. (2007) Evaluation of the control banding method – comparison with measurement-based comprehensive risk assessment. J Occup Health. 49:482-492. 10.1539/joh.49.482

165. ACGIH (2019). Industrial ventilation: A manual of recommended practice for design (30th Edition, ISBN: 9781607261087). American Conference of Governmental Industrial Hygienists. Store - Industrial Ventilation: A Manual of Recommended Practice for Design, 30th Edition - ACGIH Portal

166. HSE (2003). Spray painting (medium scale). COSHH Essentials G221. Health and Safety Executive. COSHH essentials: G221: Spray painting (medium scale) (hse.gov.uk)

167. HSE (Webpage) COSH e-tool, Getting started - COSHH e-tool (hse.gov.uk)

168. HSE. (2019) HSE risk assessment template and worked examples. Risk assessment: Template and examples - HSE

169. HSE. (2014). Introduction to LEV https://youtu.be/Ky8y2jDk6i8

170. HSE. (2016) Clearing the air. INDG408(rev1) - Clear the air: A simple guide to buying and using local exhaust ventilation (LEV) (hse.gov.uk)

171. BOHS. (2021) Basic design principles of local exhaust ventilation systems. QC.1-26-07-2021-P602-Qualification-Specification.pdf (bohs.org)

172. BOHS. (2021) Through examination and testing of local exhaust ventilation systems QC.1-26-07-2021-P602-Qualification-Specification.pdf (bohs.org)

173. BOHS. (webpage) Performance evaluation, commissioning and management of local exhaust ventilations systems. Performance Evaluation, Commissioning and Management of Local Exhaust Ventilation Systems P604 - British Occupational Hygiene Society (BOHS)

174. HSE. (2017) Determining the capture zone of a common LEV capture hood. https://youtu.be/SwM_KQRQ8aI

175. AES Ltd. (2015) Dust lamp test at wood lathe. https://youtu.be/sXtp1nm6O14

176. HSE. (2015) The dust lamp. The dust lamp: A simple tool for observing the presence of airborne particles MDHS82 (hse.gov.uk)

177. Rajan B (2021) Respiratory protective equipment. LOcHER-RPE. respirators-4-fine-tune-april-21.pptx (live.com)

178. British Safety Industry Federation (BSIF). Clean Air? Take Care? Clean air? take care! | BSIF

179. Scottish Centre for Healthy Working Lives. RPE Selector Tool. RPE selector tool - Healthy Working Lives

180. HSE (2013). Respiratory protective equipment at work: A practical guide (HSG53). Health and Safety Executive. Respiratory protective equipment at work: A practical guide HSG53 (hse.gov.uk)

181. HSE. (2005) HSE. Respiratory protective equipment at work, HSG53 (first edition, 2005). Withdrawn by HSE.

182. HSE (webpage). Skin at work. HSE: Skin at work

183. HSE. (2015) Memory aid for selecting protective gloves (HSG262). Managing skin exposure risks at work HSG262 (hse.gov.uk)

184. HSE. (2006) Monitoring strategies for toxic substances (HSG173). Monitoring strategies for toxic substances (hse.gov.uk)

185. Cherrie J, Howie R, Semple S. (2010) Monitoring for health hazards at work. Wiley-Blackwell, John Wiley & sons Ltd., London.

186. Rajan B, Llewellyn, Darnton A. (2015) Leading indicators pilot survey – Ill health Prevention Performance Indicators (IPPI). IOSH Conference 2015, London.

187. Molloy M (2021) Findings from welding fume inspection. OH2021-BOHS. OH2021 Full Programme (bohs.org)

188. Calcutt M (2021) Insights into HSE's intervention approach. OH2021-BOHS. OH2021 Full Programme (bohs.org)

189. Gantz SD. (2014) The basics of IT audit. Purposes, processes and practical information. Syngress. https://doi.org/10.1016/C2013-0-06954-X

190. Wagner H-J, Beimborn D and Weitzel T. (2014) How social capital among information technology and business units drives operational alignment and IT business value. J Management Inf. Sys; 3:1241-272. https://doi.org/10.2753/MIS0742-1222310110

191. HSE (Webpage). Measuring performance. Managing Health and Safety Performance (hse.gov.uk)

192. RoSPA. Measuring OH&S performance. Measurement and management. Measuring OS&H performance - RoSPA

193. Hasle P, Madsen CU and Hansen D. (2021) Integrating operations management and occupational health and safety: A necessary part of safety science. Safety Sci; 139: 18 pages. https://doi.org/10.1016/j.ssci.2021.105247

194. Borys D. (2014) The value proposition for the occupational health and safety professionals' literature review. International Network of Safety & Health Practitioner Organisations (INSHPO). INSHPO_OSH_prof_lit_review_online_0914.pdf

195. Tyers C, Hicks B. (2012) Occupational health provision on the Olympic Park and athletes' village. HSE Research Report RR921. RR921 - Research into Occupational Health Performance on the Olympic Park and Athletes' Village (hse.gov.uk)

196. Howells S. (2015) Why health is so beneficial at Thames tideway tunnel. Safety and Health Practitioner on line. Why health is so beneficial at Thames Tideway Tunnel - SHP - Health and Safety News, Legislation, PPE, CPD and Resources (shponline.co.uk).

197. Jones W, Gibb A. (2017) Crossrail: Occupational safety and health arrangements. Loughborough University. HS33_OSH Arrangements on Crossrail_Overview.

198. American Industrial Hygiene Association. (2015) Best practice guide for leading health metrics in occupational health and safety programmes. Best-Practice-Guide-for-Leading-Health-Metrics-in-Occupational-Health-and-Safety-Programs-Guidance-Document.pdf (aiha-assets.sfo2.digitaloceanspaces.com)

199. National Safety Council and the Campbell Institute. (2019) An implementation guid to leading indicators. Campbell-Institute-An-Implementation-Guide-to-Leading-Indicators.pdf (thecampbellinstitute.org)

200. Internal Council on Mining & Metals. (2012) Overview of leading indicators for occupational health and safety in mining. ICMM - Overview of Leading Indicators for Occupational Health and Safety in Mining

201. Occupational Safety and Health Administration (OHSA). (2019) Using leading indicators to improve safety and health outcomes. Leading Indicators | Occupational Safety and Health Administration (osha.gov)

202. Tremblay A, Badri A. (2018) Assessment of Occupational Health and Safety performance evaluation tools: state of the art and challenges for small and mediums size enterprises. Safety Science; 101: 260-267. https://doi.org/10.1016/j.ssci.2017.09.016

203. HSE. (2001) A guide to measuring health & safety performance. Guide to measuring health and safety performance (hse.gov.uk)

204. The Law Dictionary. Proxy indicator definition & legal meaning What is PROXY INDICATOR? definition of PROXY INDICATOR (Black's Law Dictionary) (thelawdictionary.org)

205. Drucker PF. (2002) The effective executive. Harper Business Essentials. Peter Drucker - The effective Executive (3).pdf (google.com)

206. BOHS. (2021) Good practice guide for consultants. Good-Practice-Guide-Version-2-rebranded-2021-1.pdf (bohs.org)

207. IOSH. (2018) Consultancy-Good practice guide. ps0353-consultancy-good-practice-guide-new.pdf (iosh.com)

208. HSE (webpage). Competence in health and safety. Competence in health and safety - HSE

209. Strong EK. (1925) Theories of Selling. J Appl. Psyc; 9: 75-86. https://doi.org/10.1037/h0070123

210. Prater M. (2018) A 10-minute summary of "The Psychology of Selling" by Brian Tracy. A 10-Minute Summary of "The Psychology of Selling" by Brian Tracy (hubspot.com)

211. BSI. (2014) Respiratory equipment: Compressed gases for breathing apparatus. BS EN 12021:2014 free download - Free Standards Download

212. HSE (Webpage). Human factors: Behavioural safety aspects (an introduction). Human factors: Behavioural safety approaches - an introduction (hse.gov.uk)

213. BBC-Bitesize (webpage). Communication. What is communication? - Communication - GCSE Business Revision - Other - BBC Bitesize

214. Education Executive (Edexec). (2017) The 7Cs of communication. The seven Cs of Communication | Edexec

215. Covello VT, Milligan PA. (2015) Risk Communication - Principles, tool & techniques. Presented at the USNRC. (Covello and Milligan - Risk Communication - Principles, Tools, & Techniques. (nrc.gov)

216. Sandman P. (2017) Three types of risk communication. Presented at the Australian Environmental Lar Enforcement and Regulation Network. Three types of risk communication- Peter Sandman on Vimeo

217. Sandman P (2013) Communicating risk: Neglected and controversial rules of thumb. Peter Sandman, Ph.D., a leading expert in health and risk communications - Bing video

218. UK Resilience. Communicating Risk. Checklists and Frameworks (publishing.service.gov.uk)

219. Thaler RH, Sunstein CR. (2021) Nudge: Final Edition. Penguin.

220. Thaler R. (2018) Richard Thaler explains his 'nudge' theory. Nobel Prize - Richard Thaler explains his 'nudge' theory - Bing video

221. Thaler R. (2011) Nudge: an overview. Richard Thaler - Nudge: An Overview - Bing video

222. Dolan P, Hallsworth M, Halpern D et al. (2010) MINDSPACE: influencing behaviour through public policy. Institute for Government. MINDSPACE | The Behavioural Insights Team (bi.team)

223. Epstein S. (1994) Integration of the cognitive and the psychodynamic unconscious. *Am J Psychol;* 49:709–24. https://doi.org/10.1037/0003-066X.49.8.709

224. Kanheman D. (2013) Thinking fast and slow. Farrar, Straus and Giroux; New York. (Reprint edition).

225. Tay SW, Ryan PM, Ryan CA. (2016) System 1 and 2 thinking processes and cognitive reflection testing in medical students. C Med Ed J; 7: 97-103. https://doi.org/10.36834/cmej.36777

Index

4Ds, 25

ACoP, 15, 26, 27, 31, 53, 63, 70, 76, 113, 146

Admin failures, 5, 66

AIDA, 15, 180, 181, 182, 183, 187

analytical mind, 197

automatic mind, 197, 199

Barbecue (smoke) effect, 128, 132

blue-tape, 174, 178, 181

BM, 159, 162, 163, 165, 166, 170

BOHS, 11, 15, 17, 19, 20, 21, 26, 34, 66, 101, 114, 205, 206, 214, 216, 217, 218, 220

breathing apparatus, 135, 220

BSIF, 11, 15, 21, 22, 136, 137, 156, 218

Building finance, 7, 181

cancer, 21, 30, 45, 83, 84, 85, 185, 207

captor hood, 96, 97, 116, 117, 128, 132

capture bubble, 74, 95, 115, 116, 117, 118, 168

capture distance indicator, 117

capture velocity, 116, 117, 133

capture zone, 6, 74, 97, 115, 116, 117, 118, 120, 132, 133, 195, 218

challenges, 14, 19, 22, 26, 46, 52, 60, 61, 65, 74, 80, 220

challenges and failures, 46, 60, 74

checks, 35, 51, 102, 137, 163, 168, 169

choice architecture, 196

chronic, 30, 57, 60, 63, 85, 161

coalface, 7, 13, 31, 38, 39, 52, 58, 60, 66, 74, 109, 110, 172, 173

commensurate, 47, 113

competence, 89, 171, 173

competency, 22, 25, 33, 36, 51, 52, 54, 63, 64, 65, 66, 68, 74, 110, 114, 126, 143, 146, 173, 174, 180, 188, 192

competent person, 38, 163, 167

confined space, 82, 163, 166

contaminant cloud, 117, 119, 120, 195

context, 19, 46, 47, 51, 59, 78, 80, 159, 161, 181, 199, 202

contexts, 46, 197, 202

control banding, 6, 57, 75, 81, 89, 101, 111, 137, 211, 216, 217

COSHH, 1, 4, 5, 6, 7, 10, 12, 13, 14, 15, 17, 18, 19, 20, 23, 26, 27, 28, 31, 32, 34, 35, 36, 38, 39, 46, 47, 48, 50, 51, 52, 53, 54, 55, 56, 57, 58, 59, 60, 61, 63, 64, 65, 66, 67, 70, 71, 73, 75, 76, 79, 81, 84, 88, 89, 90, 91, 94, 96, 97, 99, 100, 101, 103, 111, 113, 114, 118, 121, 128, 133, 135, 136, 137, 146, 153, 156, 158, 159, 160, 161, 162, 163, 164,
165, 166, 169, 171, 172, 173, 174, 177, 178, 185, 186, 196, 197, 200, 205, 206, 208, 209, 210, 211, 212, 213, 214, 215, 216, 217

COSHH awareness, 65

COSHH Essentials, 57, 75, 81, 89, 90, 91, 94, 96, 97, 99, 101, 103, 162, 186, 211, 216, 217

COSHH Essentials direct advice sheets, 5, 75, 89, 91, 94, 96, 97

COSHH-e-tool, 91

COSHH-generic ECIs, 162

COSHH-RM, 10, 13, 14, 26, 28, 38, 46, 53, 55, 57, 59, 60, 66, 73, 75, 76, 114, 159, 160, 165, 171, 177

direct advice sheets, 5, 63, 89, 91, 92, 113

Drucker, 171, 173, 220

dust, 15, 25, 26, 27, 28, 29, 31, 32, 33, 34, 35, 40, 45, 46, 57, 61, 67, 73, 80, 81, 84, 85, 86, 90, 94, 95, 96, 97, 98, 99, 105, 106, 110, 116, 118, 119, 121, 122, 127, 128, 131, 140, 141, 142, 148, 149, 151, 152, 156, 158, 162, 166, 167, 168, 185, 186, 191, 206, 210, 215, 216, 218

dust trigger values, 31, 34, 81, 127, 206

ECIs, 7, 158, 159, 160, 161, 162, 163, 164, 165, 166, 177

eddy, 117

empire building, 49, 173

empower, 5, 72

encourage, 13, 52, 54, 117, 161, 168, 203

enforcement action, 46, 48, 51

engage, 13, 18, 52, 54, 57, 81, 176, 203

essential practices, 172, 173

excessive exposure, 48, 57, 60, 133, 148, 160, 169

explain, 13, 19, 54, 61, 70, 79, 113, 133, 171, 197, 199, 203

Exposure Control Indicators, 7, 158, 159, 163

exposure likelihood, 37, 82, 85, 88

exposure monitoring, 34, 35, 51, 61, 67, 128, 158, 164, 169, 191

exposure potential, 101, 103, 105, 108

FABRIC, 14

failures, 5, 45, 53, 56, 63, 66, 69, 82, 94, 95, 98, 136, 160, 186, 214

financial terms, 7, 181, 183

foundry fume, 34, 35, 162

fume, 26, 28, 29, 31, 45, 93, 100, 124, 128, 141, 142, 152, 167, 201, 216, 218

gas, 26, 29, 81, 110, 142, 152, 163

general ventilation, 6, 33, 90, 101, 103, 106, 107, 114, 131, 132, 133, 134, 163, 168

GHS, 6, 15, 30, 127

198

gold plating, 49, 181

good practice, 4, 13, 31, 36, 37, 51, 59, 61, 72, 95, 126, 127, 128, 148, 158, 160, 169, 174, 177, 178

Hazard, 15, 30, 101, 103, 104, 107, 109

Health Risks at Work. Do you know yours?, 5, 75, 79

health surveillance, 46, 51, 61, 67, 128, 90, 164, 169, 213

Hippocrates, 4, 19, 25, 135, 204

HSE, 4, 6, 11, 12, 15, 17, 22, 31, 35, 36, 39, 40, 42, 46, 47, 49, 51, 52, 53, 54, 55, 56, 57, 58, 61, 64, 65, 66, 67, 69, 71, 72, 75, 79, 81, 82, 86, 89, 91, 93, 94, 97, 98, 100, 101, 103, 111, 112, 113, 114, 116, 121, 127, 128, 131, 137, 141, 146, 147, 153, 156, 158, 159, 160, 162, 169, 171, 172, 173, 176, 179, 182, 185, 186, 191, 192, 200, 205, 206, 207, 208, 209, 210, 211, 212, 213, 214, 215, 216, 217, 218, 219, 220

HSE risk assessment template, 112, 113, 121

HSWA, 15, 26, 205

human factors, 100, 172

inadequate 5, 46, 73, 81, 96, 118, 127, 128, 133, 140, 144, 145, 169, 170

inadvertent exposure, 148

IOM, 15, 18

IOSH, 15, 20, 216, 218, 220

isocyanate, 33, 35, 80, 81, 162, 212

lagging indicators, 53, 54, 160, 162

LEV, 6, 15, 16, 26, 35, 66, 74, 82, 89, 90, 91, 93, 94, 95, 96, 97, 98, 99, 100, 101, 106, 114, 115, 117, 118, 119, 120, 121, 124, 125, 126, 127, 129, 130, 132, 133, 135, 160, 163, 165, 166, 167, 168, 177, 183, 185, 186, 187, 189, 194, 195, 197, 200, 214, 216, 217, 218

LOcHER, 5, 13, 14, 15, 17, 72, 75, 76, 79, 80, 136, 143, 212, 213, 215, 218

LÖftstedt, 207

long latency, 60, 67

lung disease, 53, 210, 211, 215

maintenance, 35, 38, 58, 82, 90, 101, 102, 114, 121, 133, 135, 136, 137, 142, 144, 163, 165, 168, 177, 212

Make it happen, 172, 189

MINDSPACE, 199, 221

mist, 29, 31, 35, 108, 167, 197

misuse, 135, 136, 139, 144, 145

NDMs, 141, 145

NEBOSH, 15, 23

Needs of SMEs, 4, 57

nudge, 10, 13, 65, 67, 71, 88, 113, 117, 122, 124, 172, 189, 196, 197, 199, 200, 221

Occupational Safety and Health Consultants Register, 15, 50, 208

operations, 13, 34, 37, 38, 56, 60, 61, 68, 71, 72, 79, 80, 87, 95, 136, 140, 159, 179, 181, 188, 217, 219

OSH buy-in, 7, 18, 57, 71, 179, 180, 181, 185, 188

OSH salesperson, 7, 180

OSHCR, 15, 50, 173, 186, 208

OSHKE, 12, 14, 15, 28, 32, 34, 35, 38, 48, 52, 55, 56, 67, 68, 70, 71, 74, 85, 89, 91, 93, 95, 97, 98, 99, 100, 117, 118, 122, 123, 124, 125, 128, 131, 132, 136, 139, 143, 148, 149, 151, 158, 170, 189, 191, 195

paper mountain, 65, 89, 113, 169

particle sizes, 28, 29, 73

particulates, 108

Personal protective equipment
  PPE, 15

photo firm, 56

PPE, 5, 15, 19, 37, 72, 74, 92, 122, 136, 146, 147, 149, 151, 152, 153, 156, 161, 164, 168, 169, 197, 209, 219

precursors, 160

prevention, 36, 55, 64, 88, 154, 155, 159, 161, 167

principles of good control, 34

properties of airborne, 29

proportionality, 4, 13, 33, 46, 47, 48, 51, 52, 57, 59, 88, 89, 93, 108, 174, 177, 180, 207, 209

Proportionate work remains, 4, 42

proxy indicators, 161

prudence, 7, 13, 33, 52, 57, 59, 89, 93, 173, 174, 180, 189

Ramazzini, 25, 204

receiving hood, 95, 99, 119, 124, 185, 187

respirator, 82, 86, 98, 100, 109, 128, 135, 140, 142, 143, 146, 167

Respiratory protective equipment
  RPE, 16, 218

risk, 4, 5, 8, 10, 12, 13, 18, 19, 20, 23, 26, 31, 33, 35, 36, 37, 38, 46, 47, 48, 52, 53, 54, 55, 57, 58, 61, 63, 64, 66, 67, 69, 71, 73, 75, 80, 81, 82, 84, 85, 86, 87, 88, 89, 98, 110, 112, 113, 121, 128, 154, 159, 162, 166, 171, 173, 175, 176, 181, 186, 187, 189, 192, 193, 194, 195, 197, 202, 209, 212, 213, 215, 217, 221

Risk assessment (RA), 18, 19, 26, 33, 35, 48, 55, 58, 66, 75, 81, 84, 87, 89, 112, 113, 121, 162, 206, 213, 215, 217

risk communication, 13, 67, 69, 73, 181, 189, 192, 194, 195, 202, 221

risk ranking, 75, 85, 86

risk sharing, 63, 64

risk transfer, 63, 64

RM, 5, 7, 8, 12, 13, 15, 25, 33, 46, 48, 52, 53, 55, 56, 57, 59, 60, 61, 65, 69, 70, 71, 73, 75, 78, 79, 84, 85, 88, 89, 91, 98, 99, 112, 113, 118, 121, 160, 161, 162, 164, 165, 169, 174, 177, 179, 181, 182, 191, 192, 197, 199, 201, 202, 217

RoSPA, 9, 10, 11, 16, 24, 79, 214, 219

RPE selection, 6, 136, 137, 139, 145, 146, 177

RPE selector tool, 91, 137, 138, 139, 141, 218

RPE use, 6, 139, 141, 142

rules community, 174

Safe working distance
   SWD, 16, 167

Safe working load
   SWL, 16

Safety Groups UK, 16, 17, 23, 215

Schedule 2A, 36, 174

Scottish Healthy Working Lives
   SHWL, 65, 79, 137, 213

sensitisers, 30, 56, 156

serious harm, 53, 57

serious health effects, 83, 85, 113, 159

significant health effects, 84

silica dust, 26, 29, 85, 162, 185

six staircase steps, 76

skin exposure, 6, 17, 67, 97, 122, 147, 148, 149, 150, 153, 154, 155, 156, 157, 169, 196, 214, 218

skin exposure control, 154

skin exposure pathways, 150, 169

so far as is reasonably practical, 33, 53

statistics, 4, 45, 53, 60, 80, 160, 172, 179, 206, 207, 210

substances hazardous to health
   SHH, 5, 10, 17, 18, 20, 34, 37, 75, 76, 77, 205, 206, 215

substitution, 4, 32, 161, 163, 167

system 1 mind, 197

system 2 mind, 198

technology, 26, 53, 70, 154, 155, 157, 167, 172, 173, 219

TExT, 16, 160, 163, 165, 168, 187

Time weighted average, 16

tolerable, 81, 84, 136, 164, 169

TWA, 16, 31, 35, 36, 101, 158

Tyndall, 148

vapour, 26, 33, 73, 82, 106, 109, 110, 118, 120, 121, 125, 142, 151, 152, 156, 217

vapours, 28, 35, 45, 57, 100, 108, 120, 123, 141, 142, 149, 166

WEL, 16, 34, 36, 158

welding, 28, 29, 31, 57, 89, 93, 124, 166, 167, 201, 218

wood dust, 27, 141

working zone, 121, 125

workplace exposure limits, 31

work-related lung diseases, 42, 53

young, 25, 79, 88, 215

Printed in Great Britain
by Amazon

19028634R00129